MULTICULTURAL E̲

JAMES A. BANKS, *Series Editor*

(continued)

Transformative Ethnic Studies in Schools

Curriculum, Pedagogy, and Research

Christine E. Sleeter
Miguel Zavala

TEACHERS COLLEGE PRESS

TEACHERS COLLEGE | COLUMBIA UNIVERSITY
NEW YORK AND LONDON

Published by Teachers College Press, 1234 Amsterdam Avenue, New York, NY 10027

Copyright © 2020 by Teachers College, Columbia University

Book cover art design by Abd Hadi Gustavo Zavala

Library of Congress Cataloging-in-Publication Data

Names: Sleeter, Christine E., 1948– author. | Zavala, Miguel, 1972– author.
Title: Transformative ethnic studies in schools : curriculum, pedagogy, and research / Christine E. Sleeter, Miguel Zavala.
Description: New York, NY : Teachers College Press, [2020] | Series: MCE Series | Includes bibliographical references and index.
Identifiers: LCCN 2019052013 (print) | LCCN 2019052014 (ebook) | ISBN 9780807763469 (hardcover) | ISBN 9780807763452 (paperback) | ISBN 9780807778388 (ebook)
Subjects: LCSH: Ethnology—Study and teaching—United States. | Multicultural education—United States.
Classification: LCC GN307.85.U6 S54 2020 (print) | LCC GN307.85.U6 (ebook) | DDC 305.80071/073—dc23
LC record available at https://lccn.loc.gov/2019052013
LC ebook record available at https://lccn.loc.gov/2019052014

ISBN 978-0-8077-6345-2 (paper)
ISBN 978-0-8077-6346-9 (hardcover)
ISBN 978-0-8077-7838-8 (ebook)

Printed on acid-free paper
Manufactured in the United States of America

Contents

Series Foreword

Because of broken and deferred dreams for more than 3 centuries during their sojourn in America, African Americans began a quest for their rights and freedoms in the 1960s that was unprecedented in their history. Their quest culminated in the Civil Rights Movement, which gave birth to the ethnic studies movement in which African Americans and other ethnic groups (such as Mexican Americans, Asian Americans, and American Indians) demanded that school, college, and university curricula be changed to reflect their histories, cultures, hopes, and dreams. These groups were largely invisible or depicted in stereotypic images in society writ large and in the curricula of mainstream educational institutions.

The Black Studies movement, which spearheaded the ethnic studies movement that emerged in the 1960s and 1970s, built upon the seminal research and publications that had been developed by African American historians and social scientists since the late 1800s. These publications included the two-volume *History of the Negro Race in America from 1619 to 1880* by George Washington Williams (1882, 1883); *The Philadelphia Negro: A Social Study* by W.E.B. Du Bois (1899); *The Negro in Our History* by Carter G. Woodson and Charles H. Wesley (1922); and *From Slavery to Freedom: A History of Negro Americans* by John Hope Franklin (1947).

Influential publications about Mexican Americans during this first phase of ethnic studies included Carey McWilliams's *North from Mexico: The Spanish-Speaking People of the United* States (1949) and Manuel Gamio's *Mexican Immigration to the United States* (1930), a well-researched description of the first wave of Mexican immigrants to the United States. Three important scholarly books published about Filipino Americans during this period were *Filipino Immigration to the Continental United States and Hawaii* by Bruno Lasker (1931); *Brothers Under the Skin* by McWilliams (1943); and *America Is in the Heart*, the powerful and discerning autobiography by the writer Carlos Bulosan (1943).

The books and publications by African American scholars had been largely ignored by White scholars and were invisible in most mainstream academic institutions and in popular culture when the ethnic studies movement began. However, they were used extensively in Black schools, colleges, and universities. The ethnic studies movement that emerged in the 1960s and 1970s is tightly linked to the seminal and transformative scholarship that existed in minority communities before the Civil Rights Movement. This early phase contained a vital and influential component for ethnic studies in schools, which included the *Negro History Bulletin* that Woodson published for elementary and secondary school teachers (beginning in 1937) and textbooks that he wrote for their students, including *Negro Makers of History* (1928) and *The Story of the Negro Retold* (1935).

A second phase of ethnic studies in schools occurred, also in the 1960s and 1970s, when minoritized groups of color demanded that schools incorporate their histories, cultures, heroes, and heroines into the curriculum. Because schools often responded to these demands quickly and with few resources, many of the resulting changes were superficial and focused on the achievements of individuals, holidays, and discrete cultural elements such as ethnic foods and music. The National Council for the Social Studies 43rd Yearbook, *Teaching Ethnic Studies: Concepts and Strategies* (Banks, 1973), provided conceptual, content, and pedagogical assistance to teachers and school practitioners for teaching ethnic studies. I published the first edition of my book, *Teaching Strategies for Ethnic Studies*, in 1975, and it became a widely used textbook in teacher education programs in colleges of education. When the 8th edition of that book was published in 2009, the momentum and popularity of ethnic studies had waned in both colleges of education and in schools. The focus had shifted to a broader conception of diversity—multicultural education—which incorporates variables such as race, social class, gender, exceptionality, and LGBTQ issues (Banks & Banks, 2016; Sleeter & Grant, 2009).

Sleeter and Zavala's timely, engaging, and informative book marks the emergence of a third phase in the development of ethnic studies teaching and curriculum development in schools. It is difficult to determine the scope and depth of this phase in the development of school ethnic studies. However, as the authors point out, ethnic studies curriculum and courses are being developed in cities such as Philadelphia, San Francisco, Chicago, Los Angeles, Portland (Oregon), and Seattle. Most of these cities have large populations of students of color, which is probably an important reason why ethnic studies courses and curricula are being developed in those school districts. The voices and actions of students, parents, teachers, and communities of color stimulated the rise of the third phase of school ethnic studies described in this book.

This book describes a transformative and critical conception of ethnic studies, which echoes the previous work of the authors in critical theory and critical pedagogy (Sleeter, 1991; Sleeter & Delgado Bernal, 2004; Zavala, 2018). Ethnic studies is conceptualized in this book not just as a way to integrate ethnic content into the curriculum, but as a vehicle for curriculum transformation and change that will enable students to view events and issues from multiple perspectives, to critically examine structures such as institutionalized racism and inequality, and to take action to make their communities, nation, and the world more just and equitable. Another important purpose of ethnic studies described in this book is to help minoritized students understand the ways in which they have been victimized by institutionalized structures such as income inequality and racism, and to help them overcome internalized oppression. As James Baldwin incisively stated, an accurate history of racism in America liberates not only people of color but Whites as well, who also are victimized by the myths embedded within a glorified and misleading history of the United States. He wrote:

> It is not really a "Negro revolution" that is upsetting this country. What is upsetting this country is a sense of its own identity. If, for example, one managed to change the curriculum in all the schools so that [Blacks] learned more about themselves and their real contributions to this culture, you would be liberating not only [Blacks], you'd be liberating white people who know nothing about their own history. (Baldwin, 1963/1985, p. 329)

This is a propitious time to conceptualize and implement a transformative notion of ethnic studies in schools because of the increasing diversity in U.S. society and schools. American classrooms are experiencing the largest influx of immigrant students since the beginning of the 20th century. Approximately 12.6 million new immigrants—documented and undocumented—settled in the United States in the years from 2000 to 2016 (Zong, Batalova, & Hallock, 2018). Fewer than 10% came from nations in Europe. Most came from Mexico and nations in South Asia, East Asia, Latin America, the Caribbean, and Central America. The largest number of immigrants to the United States today come from India and China, not Mexico. The influence of an increasingly diverse population on U.S. schools, colleges, and universities is and will continue to be enormous.

Schools in the United States are more diverse today than they have been since the early 1900s, when a multitude of immigrants entered the United States from Southern, Central, and Eastern Europe (Banks, 2005). In 2017, the National Center for Education Statistics estimated that students from ethnic minority groups made up more than 52% of students in prekindergarten through 12th grade in U.S. public schools, an increase from 39.2% in 2001. Latinxs made up 25% of the children in the United States in 2017, African Americans were 15%, Asian and Pacific Island children were 6%, and American Indians were 1% (Annie E. Casey Foundation, 2019).

Language and religious diversity is also increasing in the U.S. student population. A Center for Migration Studies publication estimated that 21.6% of Americans aged 5 and above (65.5 million) spoke a language other than English at home in 2016 (Camarota & Ziegler, 2017). This percentage has doubled since 1990, and almost tripled since 1980. The significant number of immigrants from nations such as India and China has also increased greatly the religious diversity of the United States. Harvard professor Diana L. Eck (2001) calls the United States the "most religiously diverse nation on earth" (p. 4). Islam is now the fastest-growing religion in the United States, as well as in several European nations such as France, the United Kingdom, and the Netherlands (Banks, 2009; O'Brien, 2016).

The major purpose of the Multicultural Education Series is to provide preservice educators, practicing educators, graduate students, scholars, and policymakers with an interrelated and comprehensive set of books that summarizes and analyzes important research, theory, and practice related to the education of ethnic, racial, cultural, and linguistic groups in the United States, as well as mainstream students, about diversity. The dimensions of multicultural education, developed by Banks (2004) and described in the *Handbook of Research on Multicultural Education* and in the *Encyclopedia of Diversity in Education* (Banks, 2012), provide the conceptual framework for the development of the publications in the Series. The dimensions are content integration, the knowledge construction process, prejudice reduction, equity pedagogy, and an empowering institutional culture and social structure. The books in the Multicultural Education Series provide research, theoretical, and practical knowledge about the behaviors and learning characteristics of students of color (Conchas & Vigil, 2012; C. D. Lee, 2007), language-minority students (Gándara & Hopkins, 2010; Valdés, 2001; Valdés, Capitelli, & Alvarez, 2011), low-income students (Cookson, 2013; Gorski, 2018), and other minoritized population groups, such as students who speak different varieties of English (Charity Hudley & Mallinson, 2011) and LGBTQ youth (Mayo, 2014). A number of the books in the Multicultural Education Series focus on the nature of culturally responsive teaching (Gay, 2018; Howard, 2010), as well as on how it is implemented in content areas such as music (Campbell, 2018), science (Lee & Buxton, 2010), literacy (Lee, 2007), and mathematics (Nasir, Cabana, Shreve, Woodbury, & Louie, 2014).

This book conceptualizes ethnic studies not only as a vehicle to reform and revitalize school curricula but also as a way to transform teaching. Sleeter and Zavala state that an ethnic studies pedagogy is culturally responsive and helps students attain the knowledge, skills, and motivation to question and challenge the social, political, and economic structures within their communities and the nation. Ethnic studies pedagogy incorporates the rich cultural contexts of the communities in which students are embedded. The authors state that ethnic studies is "an anti-racist, decolonial project that seeks to rehumanize education for students of color, center subjugated knowledge narratives and ancestral knowledge, and build solidarity across racial and ethnic differences for the purpose of working toward social justice" (p. 103). The authors also view civic and social action as an important component of ethnic studies teaching and learning. These are important and ambition goals for ethnic studies teaching and, as the authors point out, will require deep knowledge, skills, and self-reflection by teachers to make them a reality. Consequently, transformative teacher education is required in order to implement the visionary conception of ethnic studies that is described in this timely, engaging, and compelling book. This book marks a new phase in the development of teaching ethnic studies in schools. I hope it will have the wide influence that it deserves.

—James A. Banks

REFERENCES

Annie E. Casey Foundation. (2019). *2019 kids count data book: State trends in child well-being*. Baltimore, MD: Author.

Baldwin, J. (1985). A talk to teachers. In J. Baldwin, *The price of the ticket: Collected nonfiction, 1948–1985* (pp. 325–332). New York, NY: St. Martin's Press. (Original work published 1963)

Banks, C.A.M. (2005). *Improving multicultural education: Lessons from the intergroup education movement*. New York, NY: Teachers College Press.

Banks, J. A. (Ed.). (1973). *Teaching ethnic studies: Concepts and strategies* (43rd yearbook). Washington, DC: National Council for the Social Studies.

Banks, J. A. (1975). *Teaching strategies for ethnic studies*. Boston, MA: Allyn & Bacon.

Banks, J. A. (2004). Multicultural education: Historical development, dimensions, and practice. In J. A. Banks & C.A.M. Banks (Eds.), *Handbook of research on multicultural education* (2nd ed., pp. 3–29). San Francisco, CA: Jossey-Bass.

Banks, J. A. (Ed.). (2009). *The Routledge international companion to multicultural education*. New York, NY, & London, UK: Routledge.

Banks, J. A. (2012). Multicultural education: Dimensions of. In J. A. Banks (Ed.), *Encyclopedia of diversity in education* (Vol. 3, pp. 1538–1547). Thousand Oaks, CA: Sage.

Banks, J. A., & Banks, C.A.M. (Eds.). (2016). *Multicultural education: Issues and perspectives* (9th ed.). Hoboken, NJ: Wiley.

Bulosan, C. (1943). *America is in the heart*. New York, NY: Harcourt.

Camarota, S. A., & Ziegler, K. (2017, October). 65.5 million U.S. residents spoke a foreign language at home in 2016. *Center for Immigration Studies*. Retrieved from cis.org/Report/655-Million-US-Residents-Spoke-Foreign-Language-Home-2016

Campbell, P. S. (2018). *Music, education, and diversity: Building cultures and communities*. New York, NY: Teachers College Press.

Charity Hudley, A. H., & Mallinson, C. (2011). *Understanding language variation in U.S. schools*. New York, NY: Teachers College Press.

Conchas, G. Q., & Vigil, J. D. (2012). *Streetsmart schoolsmart: Urban poverty and the education of adolescent boys*. New York, NY: Teachers College Press.

Cookson, P. W., Jr. (2013). *Class rules: Exposing inequality in American high schools*. New York, NY: Teachers College Press.

Du Bois, W.E.B. (2007). *The Philadelphia Negro: A social study*. Whitefish, MT: Kessinger Publishing. (Original work published 1899)

Eck, D. L. (2001). *A new religious America: How a "Christian country" has become the world's most religiously diverse nation*. New York, NY: HarperSanFrancisco.

Franklin, J. H. (1947). *From slavery to freedom: A history of Negro Americans*. New York, NY: Knopf.

Gamio, M. (1930). *Mexican immigration to the United States: A study of human migration and adjustment*. Chicago, IL: University of Chicago Press.

Gándara, P., & Hopkins, M. (Eds.). (2010). *Forbidden language: English language learners and restrictive language policies*. New York, NY: Teachers College Press.

Gay, G. (2018). *Culturally responsive teaching: Theory, research, and practice* (3rd ed.). New York, NY: Teachers College Press.

Gorski, P. C. (2018). *Reaching and teaching students in poverty: Strategies for erasing the opportunity* gap (2nd ed.). New York, NY: Teachers College Press.

Howard, T. C. (2010). *Why race and culture matter in schools: Closing the achievement gap in America's classrooms.* New York, NY: Teachers College Press.

Lasker, B. (1931). *Filipino immigration to the continental United States and Hawaii.* Chicago, IL: University of Chicago Press.

Lee, C. D. (2007). *Culture, literacy, and learning: Taking bloom in the midst of the whirlwind.* New York, NY: Teachers College Press.

Lee, O., & Buxton, C. A. (2010). *Diversity and equity in science: Research, policy, and practice.* New York, NY: Teachers College Press.

Mayo, C. (2014). *LGBTQ youth and education: Policies and practices.* New York, NY: Teachers College Press.

McWilliams, C. (1943). *Brothers under the skin.* Boston, MA: Little, Brown.

McWilliams, C. (1949). *North from Mexico: The Spanish-speaking people of the United States.* Philadelphia, PA: Lippincott.

Nasir, N. S., Cabana, C., Shreve, B., Woodbury, E., & Louie, N. (Eds.). (2014). *Mathematics for equity: A framework for successful practice.* New York, NY: Teachers College Press.

National Center for Education Statistics. (2017). *Enrollment and percentage distribution of enrollment in public elementary and secondary schools, by race/ethnicity and region: Selected years, fall 1995 through fall 2025.* Retrieved from nces.ed.gov/programs/digest/d15/tables/dt15_203.50.asp

O'Brien, P. (2016). *The Muslim question in Europe: Political controversies and public philosophies.* Philadelphia, PA: Temple University Press.

Sleeter, C. E. (Ed.). (1991). *Empowerment through multicultural education.* Albany, NY: State University of New York Press.

Sleeter, C. E., & Delgado Bernal, D. (2004). Critical pedagogy, critical race theory, and antiracist education: Implications for multicultural education. In J. A. Banks & C.A.M. Banks (Eds.), *Handbook of research on multicultural education* (2nd ed., pp. 240–258). San Francisco, CA: Jossey-Bass.

Sleeter, C. E., & Grant, C. A. (2009). *Making choices for multicultural education: Five approaches to race, class, and gender* (6th ed.). Hoboken, NJ: Wiley.

Valdés, G. (2001). *Learning and not learning English: Latino students in American schools.* New York, NY: Teachers College Press.

Valdés, G., Capitelli, S., & Alvarez, L. (2011). *Latino children learning English: Steps in the journey.* New York, NY: Teachers College Press.

Williams, G. W. (1968). *History of the Negro race in America from 1619–1880.* New York, NY: Arno Press. (Original work published 1882 and 1883)

Woodson, C. G. (1928). *Negro makers of history.* Washington, DC: The Associated Publishers.

Woodson, C. G. (1935). *The story of the Negro retold.* Washington, DC: The Associated Publishers.

Woodson, C. G., & Wesley, C. H. (1922). *The Negro in our history.* Washington, DC: The Associated Publishers.

Zavala, M. (2018). *Raza struggle and the movement for ethnic studies: Decolonial pedagogies, literacies, and methodologies.* New York, NY: Peter Lang.

Zong, J., Batalova, J., & Hallock, J. (2018, July 10). Frequently requested statistics on immigrants and immigration in the United States. *The Migration Policy Institute.* Retrieved from migrationpolicy.org/article/frequently-requested-statistics-immigrants-and-immigration-united-states#Demographic

Acknowledgments

We wish to thank several people without whom this book might not have happened. We are very grateful to James Banks for encouraging us to expand on our work in ethnic studies, turning it into a book. We are indebted to his deep interest, along with his helpful feedback on our thinking as we conceptualized the book, and his feedback on an earlier draft. Given his own groundbreaking work in ethnic studies, reflected in *Teaching Strategies for Ethnic Studies*, now in its 8th edition, we humbly appreciate his interest in seeing our book through to publication.

Brian Ellerbeck, our esteemed editor at Teachers College Press, was a firm source of encouragement and feedback. Brian has an eye that is exceptionally well-tuned to the market in education, as well as a keen sense of writing that has social value. We much appreciate his work in seeing this book through, from initial conception to publication.

We are most grateful to Curtis Acosta and David Stovall for their feedback on an earlier draft of this book. Their suggestions enriched the book; they also affirmed our thinking about ideas we hoped we were getting right. Two anonymous reviewers of the book's prospectus provided us with several very helpful suggestions; we hope we did justice to them.

The teachers, scholars, and activists who allowed us to enter their professional worlds through interviews played a huge role in making this book what it is. We thank them deeply for the time and wisdom they shared with us. For us, each interview was an exciting and valuable learning experience, and through their voices our readers will continue to be inspired.

Finally, we would be remiss if we did not acknowledge the groundbreaking foundational work of the Mexican American Studies teachers in Tucson. The highly impactful and inspirational program they built laid valuable groundwork for ethnic studies in K–12 schools now. We hope this book does justice to the loving and visionary work of those teachers.

CHAPTER 1

What Is All This Fuss About Ethnic Studies?

A STORY OF SCHOOLING AND THE LEGACIES OF COLONIALISM

Amarilis is now a 4th-grade student who has enrolled in five public elementary schools. Her parents are themselves intergenerational working-class Mexican Americans. Dissatisfied with the way schools have treated Amarilis, her parents have navigated different schools and districts with the hope of finding classrooms that respect the development of children. Her parents recall several incidents that led to moving her to a different school. Ever since enrolling Amarilis in her first dual-immersion-language program, they were shocked by the high number of students in the classroom. At 36 students per classroom and no instructional aide, teachers in the district, which serves economically challenged and racially diverse students, clearly were overworked and could not meet the needs of students like Amarilis, who were already framed at such a young age as "being behind" in reading and mathematics. In meetings with teachers and principals it became evident to Amarilis's parents that a culture of standards and test preparation had greatly eroded time for social role-play, nap time, and recess for kindergartners and 1st-graders.

Perhaps the most telling part of this story is not so much the negative impact of a standards-based and testing culture on young children's educational experiences, but the insidious ways in which the curriculum fosters complacency and "American" perspectives that do not represent children like Amarilis. For instance, Amarilis came home one day with a set of readings about slavery in the United States. While her parents were pleased this topic was being addressed, the assignments and readings portrayed African American heroes and heroines of the time without a critical assessment of slavery, its genesis, or how it had come to profoundly shape the lives of African Americans today. Moreover, the unit on slavery conveyed a message of racial integration and a peaceful and happy multicultural society "that represents our country today."

Fast-forward to 3rd grade. Amarilis's parents were shocked when the series of chapters on "America's Past" in the context of the U.S. Southwest literally described English colonists, such as Sir Francis Drake, as major California "pioneers." The next chapter of this district-adopted textbook skipped over a critical 200-year period, jumping from 1650 to the 1850s. The text made absolutely no mention of California Native Americans (if they appeared at all, it was in the initial chapter on "Flora and Fauna and Tribes"), much less the fact that California was Mexican land, or how the United States acquired such a vast territory.

In 4th grade, Amarilis was assigned a California missions project, which asked students to "write a report by visiting a California mission or to build a replica of a mission." In the readings and instructions for this missions project, which was framed as a significant part of the semester grade and to which the teacher dedicated 4 weeks of instruction, nowhere was there any reference to racial conflict or the treatment of Native Americans by Spanish missionaries. The entire project was literally ahistorical, focusing on the missions' architectural structures and on reproducing a tourist-brochure rendition of the past, thus erasing the atrocities committed against Native peoples.

Amarilis's early experience with social studies is not just one of histori-cal omission; our concern is with the ways Eurocentric renditions of history devalue the perspectives of marginalized communities and the impact this has on a child's sense of self, as well as how it negatively undermines stu-dents' racial literacies. As a young Chicana who experiences a world—both inside and outside school—as thoroughly racialized and conflict-ridden, these superficial lessons do not equip Amarilis with the vital tools needed for critically understanding and responding to burning questions she has raised to her parents: "Why are African Americans killed by the police?" "Why does Trump hate Mexicans?" "Are all White people bad?" Like many other families of color, Amarilis's parents felt the need to supplement the curric-ulum with their own family history. In the California missions project, for instance, Amarilis's parents assisted her with taking on the project from a Native American perspective rather than the seemingly neutral stance the instructions asked students to assume.

To understand Amarilis's story, which is common to thousands of chil-dren daily, it's necessary to grasp the historical context that has shaped schooling in the United States. Absent this contextualization, the tendency is to minimize the psychological and social impact of a Eurocentric curriculum or to render its presence invisible altogether and thus continue to perpetuate racism in our schools and our society.

Without a doubt, White settler colonialism has been a major force that not only defines but also sets the conditions for schooling as it appears today. While many frame schools as democratic institutions, we are keen here not to propagate myopic understandings that sever education from the histories of colonialism (and later capitalist development)—but we also are cautious not to subscribe to overdeterministic readings that render schools as uncontested and mere instruments of social and economic domination. Assuming a critical, historical accounting of schooling in the United States in the context of White settler colonialism, we are reminded of the social histories of racial apartheid and how these have come to shape both the curriculum and schooling structures. For instance, the legacy of segregated schools in the South and Southwest, premised on racial housing covenants that set boundaries separating White and non-White (i.e., Black and Mexican) spaces, has had a profound impact on Black, Brown, and other communities of color. This form of residential and school segregation, while challenged in the courts, especially in the historic 1954 *Brown v. Board of Education* court case decision decrying "separate but equal" as unconstitutional, remains a matter of fact, a *de facto* practice marked by predominantly White suburbs and Black and Brown urban centers. This racial divide has been perpetuated by such practices as tracking and ability grouping, differential access to college-going courses, distinct teacher expectations, school-funding disparities, and curricular differentiation. But perhaps the most oppressive aspect of a colonizing education is the way in which it functions to deculturalize, by "destroying a people's culture (cultural genocide) and replacing it with a new culture" (Spring, 2016, p. 8). Spring traces the institutionalization of deculturalization to the late 1700s with the advent of boarding schools designed to "civilize" Native American children. We believe deculturalization did not end with boarding schools and has become a fundamental aspect of schooling in the United States.

White supremacy, Native erasure, Black enslavement, Chicano subjugation in the Southwest, Asian invisibility—the broader tapestry of otherness in the context of Eurocentrism—have come to fuel these colonizing processes. European settlers introduced ideas of racial difference and superiority, which positioned Native American peoples and Black slaves as subhuman, thus justifying genocide, land dispossession, enslavement, and exploitation of non-Europeans throughout the United States and the Americas. Colonial domination, also characterized as *coloniality* (see Mignolo, 2012) to signal its continuation, has been carried forward through epistemic genocide. Epistemic genocide can be defined as the process of exterminating cultural traditions and ways of knowing. Historically, this has manifested in terms of forced assimilation into the dominant culture, language, and traditions. Schools, along with other institutions, have become major vehicles for cultural domination and the erasure of epistemic diversity. The logic of epistemic genocide operates at various levels and has appeared in schools as forced assimilation to European languages, the hegemony of a Eurocentric curriculum, and the normalization of Whiteness.

ETHNIC STUDIES AS A DECOLONIZING, UNFINISHED PROJECT

Ethnic studies seeks to rehumanize experiences, challenge problematic Euro-centric narratives, and build community solidarity across difference. Ethnic studies can be framed as anti-racist in the sense that it attempts to unpack, challenge, and eradicate racism as it takes place in our schools and in the broader society. But ethnic studies attempts to do more than this. Ethnic studies can be framed as part of a broader process of decolonization or "delinking that leads to de-colonial epistemic shift and brings to the fore-ground other epistemologies, other principles of knowledge and under-standing and, consequently, other economy, other politics, other ethics" (Mignolo, 2007, p. 453). Native scholars critique appropriating a language of "decolonization" that leaves White settler colonialism and the logic of Native erasure untouched: "Decolonization from settler colonialism in the US will require a repatriation of Indigenous land and abolition of slavery in all its forms" (Smith, Tuck, & Yang, 2018, p. x). As an unfinished project, ethnic studies must move toward returning what has been stolen, particularly Native lands and African American labor.

Thus, ethnic studies is not just a constellation of education projects. Rather, it is a set of political projects and emergent movements, rooted in place-based struggles over the curriculum, as communities fight for an education that is culturally relevant and responsive to their needs, interests, aspirations, and dreams. Ethnic studies, located mainly within public schools and universities, navigates a tension between liberation movements and colonial, capitalist institutions.

Ethnic studies is not a unitary movement, but rather draws strength from the differential spaces of struggle, with convergence and common ground around the fight against colonial logics of racial otherness and epistemic genocide. Schooling is a process that is lived, not just experienced cognitively. Schooling is thus engraved in students' bodies and memories. Students of color, in particular, understand, albeit to different degrees, the ways in which race and racialization operate—the ways in which they are marked based on their skin color, language, and cultural ways of being. But it is precisely this ongoing process of re-colonization, which Speed (2017) identifies as the "ongoing European American 'rightful' occupation and continued subjugation of nonwhite others" (p. 789), that generates the con-tradictions for the movements we are seeing today.

As we elaborate in Chapter 2, students' demands for ethnic studies, while they may be context-specific, grow out of their need to belong, to see themselves in the curriculum, and to be respected as human beings. Precisely because of the ongoing colonization and struggle against it, the movement (or movements) for ethnic studies can be characterized as generative, as developing in nonlinear and nonunitary ways, and as unfinished. To define unfinishedness we draw upon Freire's (2000) conceptualizations of history as possibility and Grosfoguel's (2012) translation of transmodernity as "the utopian project for the fulfillment, not of modernity or postmodernity, but rather of the incomplete and unfinished project of decolonization" (p. 86). Grosfoguel argues for an ethnic studies that draws upon "the epistemic diversity of the world . . . offering to think 'from' and 'with' those 'others' subalternized and inferiorized by Eurocentered modernity, offering to define their questions, their problems, and their intellectual dilemmas 'from' and 'with' those same racialized groups" (p. 88).

EPISTEMIC PRIVILEGE: PROPELLING THE MOVEMENT FORWARD

Standpoint theorists contend that one's social location and marginality can be transformed into a resource for social transformation. Being and seeing from the margins can give people of color, women, and other marginalized groups a particular "epistemic privilege" (Harding, 2004). The notion of epistemic privilege is exemplified in the "unique voice of color" thesis articulated by critical race scholars:

> Because of their different histories and experiences with oppression, black, American Indian, Asian, and Latinx writers and thinkers may be able to communicate to their white counterparts matters that the whites are unlikely to know. Minority status, in other words, brings with it a presumed competence to speak about race and racism. (Delgado & Stefancic, 2017, p. 11)

Rocco, Bernier, and Bowman (2014) add, "Both people of color and Whites experience race; however, for people of color, the experience is typically from the perspective of the oppressed and for Whites, it is from the perspective of oppressor. When a space is made to hear the unique voices of people of color, hope for dialogue and improved racial relations is created" (p. 461).

For educators, students, cultural workers, and scholar-activists who see themselves as part of the movement for ethnic studies, these insights about the privileged position that minoritized voices hold prompt us to ask fundamental questions about the potential of ethnic studies not just in re-centering nondominant perspectives and knowledge traditions—that is, not just in replacing the Eurocentric curriculum with one that is "non"-Eurocentric—but in setting the conditions for de-linking from colonial domination. Yet, as bell hooks (1989) reminds us, the journey of naming and reclaiming who we are is a space of healing and radical opening: "We are transformed, individually, collectively, as we make radical creative space which affirms and sustains our subjectivity, which gives us a new location from which to articulate our sense of the world" (p. 23).

As ethnic studies has matured, epistemologies have been developed around the most significant ways to understand and address the concerns of historically marginalized communities. For example, Macías explains that the issue is not curricular separatism, but rather reorganizing knowledge and research processes around questions that are central to the well-being of communities of color:

> We're not talking about Chicana/o history, Chicano sociology, Chicano education, Chicano political science, Chicano literature, etc. We are talking about different topical, thematic, problem, situational sets within the studies of Chicana/o studies communities, in the United States and throughout the Americas, that has to be driven by its own visions, its own view of itself in the future, and its own methodologies. (in Rangel, 2007, p. 198)

It is thus that the potential of subjugated knowledges can propel the movement forward, as a way to reclaim what has been lost and create something new that we hope ruptures the colonizing logics of racial other-ness: "The sheer variety of colonial and neocolonial formations has necessitated fugitive socialities, or ways of living, being, and relating that have taken flight from the dominant and can only be glimpsed in fleeting moments" (Elia et al., 2016, p. 13). Seeking and learning through fugitive socialities, the multiple struggles for ethnic studies "gesture to the alternative futures that various moments and projects of anticolonialism and decolonization have attempted to chart and might still realize" (p. 13).

ETHNIC STUDIES IN OUR SCHOOLS

Ethnic studies is often taken up by school districts in an effort to academically engage and raise the achievement of students of color. While the ethnic studies programs and practices that have been studied do accomplish that aim, as we show in Chapter 3, the purpose of ethnic studies goes much deeper. Academic disengagement reflects students' responses to what happens (or fails to happen) in classrooms. As San Pedro (2018a) explains, traditional schooling "props up Whiteness as a benchmark for what society ought to be" (p. 1210). From what is taught (and students are tested on), to who teaches, to the nature of relationships that are valued, to the ways of learning that are used, to the relationship between learning and schools' community contexts—in most schools these reflect how White people see things: as master narratives that render Whiteness invisible to White students, yet highly visible to students of color.

Hu-DeHart (2004) explained that the objective of ethnic studies is "systematically examining and dismantling racism" (p. 874). This objective implies both dismantling the various forms of racism that are a part of how conventional education is structured, as well as studying the institutionalization of racism and colonialism in this country for the purpose of challenging it. Ethnic studies seeks to humanize the classroom for students of color, who have a history of experiencing dehumanization through silencing of their identities, perspectives, and intellectual abilities. Au, Brown, and Calderón (2016) poignantly state: "What we must know as peoples of color—what we must know to survive, to understand who (and where) we are, to imagine freer and more joyful futurities—demands curricula that honor the knowledge production of our ancestors; engage the yearnings of our children, families, and communities; and interrogate the enduring tradition of White supremacist subjugation and misrepresentation" (p. 151).

San Pedro (2018a) posits that ethnic studies frees space in which students can learn and teach multiple truths about their lives and realities. Ethnic studies "would require that both teachers and students have a chance to face our nation's painful past, to see how we operate within settler colonial states in order to counter that which is within and around us to seek solutions to our intersecting problems" (p. 1223). It would "center pedagogies and curriculum on the rich heritage and cultural practices that students bring with them to school" (San Pedro, 2018b, p. 334). By teaching students to actually hear one another's realities, ethnic studies is radically humanizing and aims to dismantle the gulf between oppressor and oppressed by taking on oppressive relationships themselves. In addition, ethnic studies seeks to reverse the assimilationist mission of schooling by focusing on restorative and culturally sustaining experiences that, in the words of Alim and Paris (2017), serve "to perpetuate and foster—to sustain—linguistic, literate, and cultural pluralism" (p. 1).

HALLMARKS OF ETHNIC STUDIES

Based on our familiarity with ethnic studies projects as well as the ethnic studies literature, we identified seven hallmarks of ethnic studies, summarized in Figure 1.1, that inform the rest of this book. While most projects probably do not clearly embody all seven hallmarks, most do embody several of them. Taken together, they help to distinguish strong from weak instantiations of ethnic studies.

Curriculum as Counter-Narrative

Ethnic studies reframes the narrative of school knowledge around counter-narratives of communities of color. This reframing contrasts with what schools usually do, which is to add bits of knowledge to the dominant narrative. For example, consider how schools wrestle with what to teach during Black History Month. While schools commonly use this month to recognize and teach about African Americans, exactly what they select to teach often

Figure 1.1. Hallmarks of Ethnic Studies

Curriculum as Counter-Narrative

    Curriculum from the perspectives of people of color

Criticality

    Structural analysis of racism and colonialism that works toward dismantling
    multiple forms of oppression

Reclaiming Cultural Identities

    Deep knowledge of where students come from that challenges deculturalizing
    processes; learning about the historical contributions of their communities

Intersectionality and Multiplicity

    Attending to students' multiple social identities and their positions within
    intersecting relations of power

Community Engagement

    Community-based pedagogies and experiences that bridge classrooms to
    community and social movements

Pedagogy That Is Culturally Responsive and Mediated

    Drawing upon students' lived experiences and sociocultural environments;
    intentional design of learning spaces

Students as Intellectuals

    Respecting and fostering students' curiosity, thinking, and intellectualism

---

fits White rather than Black sensibilities. In a critique of K–12 Black history
curriculum, King and Brown (2014) enumerate "problematic examples":

> A North Carolina elementary school wanting students to dress in "African Am-
> erican" attire or like a safari African animal . . . ; a Los Angeles elementary
> school's Black History Month parade featuring Black people such as Dennis
> Rodman, O. J. Simpson, and Rupaul as quintessential figures of Black history
> . . . ; and the Virginia ninth grade Black student who was made to read and
> perform Tupac and a Langston Hughes' poem, *The Ballad of the Landlord*,
> and was chastised because according to his teacher, his articulations were not
> authentically "Black enough." (p. 24)

Also problematic is the view of ethnic studies as teaching "about" diverse racial and ethnic groups, following a "group of the month" or "group
of the week" approach. The problem here is the framing of ethnic or racial
groups as "Others" who may be gazed upon, but remain silent. For example, students may complete a week-long unit about Vietnamese Americans,
or Woodland Indians, without gaining any insight into how members of

these broad categories of people define themselves or the world around them, without interacting with the people who are being studied, without historical analysis of power relations impacting the group, and without disrupting the White worldview that dominates curriculum as a whole.

As we show in more detail in subsequent chapters, school knowledge conveys a perspective or narrative about the world that makes unjust power relations appear natural. This occurs through varied processes, including presenting White narratives to the exclusion of anyone else's or, more commonly, representing diverse racial and ethnic groups within White narratives so as to appear inclusive and universal. But dominant White narratives erase the experiences and knowledge of peoples over whom White people exert control. So a unit "about" Woodland Indians might refer to colonization in the past, yet gloss over how the U.S. government and its military forcibly claimed Indigenous land to give to White settlers, how genocide was enacted and experienced, how the diverse peoples clustered under the term *Woodland Indians* made sense of life before colonization, or how Indigenous peoples continue to resist ongoing colonization today.

Ethnic studies rewrites curriculum from the perspectives of people who have been oppressed by racism and/or colonization, grounding curriculum in counter-narratives that offer historical accounts and interpretations that question dominant narratives. This is what has come to be known as *standpoint* or sociohistorical positionality, which is tied to how we see the world both as individuals and also as a collective and emergent consciousness. Au (2012) argued that the concept of "curriculum standpoint" enables educators to reflect upon the deeply rooted and contested consciousness and knowledge traditions reflected in any curriculum. As Banks (2004) explains, "The knowledge that emanates from marginalized epistemological communities often contests existing political, economic, and educational practices and calls for fundamental change and reform. It often reveals the inconsistency between the democratic ideals within a society and its social arrangements and educational practices" (p. 237).

A growing movement within ethnic studies is to re-root curriculum in ancestral knowledge traditions and epistemologies that existed prior to European colonization of the Americas. Quijano (2007) explains that the physical violence of colonization was followed by "colonization of the imagination of the dominated" (p. 169), in which Europeans repressed local cultural memories, replacing them as strongly as possible with European culture. While Indigeneity is a contested concept and practice, witnessed presently in the debates around who gets to be "Native" and whether "immigrants" are also "settler" others, particular communities have struggled for a curriculum that centers on their ancestral ways of knowing. This project of re-rooting is about ancestral, Indigenous knowledge traditions that, in the context of the United States, existed prior to European colonization. Learning about ancestral knowledges and reclaiming them can be an arduous task, as voluminous historical records and documents have been burned, destroyed, or lost. Yet oral traditions have remained, and not all documents were destroyed. These oral histories and scant artifacts kept by elders, as well as the ongoing struggle to maintain traditions even after the ongoing process of European colonization and Indigenous erasure, have become significant resources for reclaiming ancestral knowledges and in constituting ethnic studies projects.

For example, the Xicanx Institute on Teaching and Organizing (XITO) is grounded in Indigenous-*Mexica* epistemology. Its decolonizing pedagogy and curriculum are based in the *Nahui Ollin* (Four Movements), which is a core concept in *Mexica* epistemology, or what some have conceptualized as Meso-American, pre-Columbus culture. In yet another example, Africana studies scholars work to extricate Black knowledge from its colonial, Eurocentric underpinnings, and re-root it within ancestral African knowledge systems, such as early Egyptian culture dating back to 4000 B.C. (Bakari, 1997). For the K–12 level, such re-rooting seeks to connect students with precolonial knowledge systems of their ancestors.

Criticality

Ethnic studies takes a critical stance. Bohman (2005) explained that "a theory is critical to the extent that it seeks human emancipation." Criticality—a stance that seeks knowledge that helps to liberate people from oppressive circumstances—generally arises in "connection with the many social movements that identify varied dimensions of the domination of human beings." Criticality questions unjust power relations. With reference to Black studies, for example, King (2005) explained that, given the

> inherent liberatory potential of Black education, the ultimate object . . . is the universal problem of human freedom. That is, a goal of transformative education and research practice in Black education is the production of knowledge and understanding people need to rehumanize the world by dismantling hegemonic structures that impede such knowledge. (p. 5)

Dismantling hegemonic structures requires naming them, questioning their existence, and then envisioning and working toward alternatives. Racism generally is not mentioned, or barely mentioned, in mainstream curricula, yet has been foundational to U.S. society since its inception. Ethnic studies not only names racism, but probes into its foundations, its everyday workings, and its connections with capitalism, colonialism, and heteropatriarchy. Ethnic studies explicitly helps young people recognize and analyze racism for the purpose of challenging it and working toward racial justice.

In the context of a dialogue with Paulo Freire, Leistyna (2004) noted that critical consciousness "is the ability to analyze, problematize (pose questions), and affect the sociopolitical, economic, and cultural realities that shape our lives" (p. 17). He went on to explain, "For Freire, this process of transformation requires praxis and dialogue. *Praxis* refers to the ongoing relationship between theoretical understanding and critique of society and action that seeks to transform individuals and their environments" (p. 17). While Freire did not write about ethnic studies per se, his work on problem-posing education for development of critical consciousness and action helps teachers envision engaging their students in knowledge for liberation.

Criticality implies that in ethnic studies classrooms students pose questions about manifestations of oppression in their own lives, and that their questions are taken seriously. This is very different from a pedagogy that treats students as passive consumers of knowledge, even when that knowledge critiques racism. Criticality in the context of ethnic studies implies teaching students to use analytical frameworks that have arisen from those who have been marginalized by race, in order to unpack their own questions about why oppressive social relations exist and how they can be (and historically have been) challenged.

Reclaiming Cultural Identities

Many ethnic studies teachers see identity work as a core practice of ethnic studies. While developing students' critical understanding of themselves, their histories, and their futures is vital to ethnic studies projects, ethnic studies that does not center students' cultural identities gains little traction and thus becomes an "academic" exercise, as currently is experienced in traditional approaches to social studies.

The legacies of colonialism and institutionalized forms of racism have accomplished one thing relating to identity: Students have been deculturalized (Spring, 2016), and thus stripped of their racial/ethnic identities. This process, albeit a deliberate project of colonization, has manifested in various forms, from replacing the names and original languages of individuals and communities, to delinking them from their histories and cultural practices—a process Valenzuela (2010) termed subtractive schooling. Through the curriculum, teaching, and social arrangements within classrooms and schools, a dominant culture is reproduced. Rather than beginning with students' cultural worlds and the resources they already bring to classroom spaces, subtractive schooling functions within a deficit framing that views students' backgrounds as problems at best and as practices of erasure at worst.

To note, students from dominant cultural groups also undergo deculturalization. While not in the same ways as minoritized students, White students' families have experienced cultural erasure, resulting in a White monoculture. Thus, it's not uncommon for students from European backgrounds whose families have been in the United States for generations to see themselves as "Americans" yet be disconnected from the cultural and geographic histories of their ancestors. In many instances "Whiteness" has become a monocultural practice that is not only performed among historically marginalized groups, but also impacts European-descent students.

Given the harmful and dehumanizing process of deculturalizing students, of stripping them of their cultural identities, ethnic studies teachers work to repair some of this damage by reclaiming those things that have been taken away from them. A major strategy in this regard has been to transform the curriculum in such a way that students both challenge universal (and Eurocentric) notions of who they are as "Americans" or as "immigrant" others, and also learn about the contributions of their ancestors as well as who their ancestors were. Another strategy includes challenging subtractive schooling practices by creating spaces of hope and validation, where students' familial and community histories become a starting point for students' learning.

Intersectionality and Multiplicity

Rather than conceptualizing identities as fixed and essentialized, ethnic studies probes intersectionality and multiplicity. Consider who may be viewed as Asian American. The umbrella term *Asian American* includes people of widely differing national origins who have immigrated under vastly different circumstances, for example, as refugees, as "cheap" labor, or as wealthy entrepreneurs. Asian Americans also differ by gender, sexual orientation, religion, ancestral language(s), (dis)ability, and so forth. Their multiplicity does not negate "Asian American" as meaningful, but it cautions against oversimplification, as well as replication of power dynamics such as patriarchy.

McCall (2005) defined intersectionality as "the relationships among multiple dimensions and modalities of social relations and subject formations" (p. 1771). Although ethnic studies centers its analysis on race and racism, an intersectional approach also attends to students' multiple social identities and their positions within intersecting relations of power. All of us embody multiple identities, which some refer to as "microcultures" (Neuliep, 2008). In addition to identifying by race/ethnicity, each of us has a gender identity, a geographic identity, a language identity, a national identity, and so forth.

Social identities are located within relations of power. Structural intersectionality "refers to the connectedness of systems and structures in society and how those systems affect individuals and groups differently" (Few-Demo, 2014, p. 171). Racism intersects with capitalism; it is virtually impossible to consider one in isolation from the other. Racism also intersects with patriarchy: Women of color experience racism in different ways from men of color. Crenshaw (1989) explained, for example, that Black women's marginalization is "greater than the sum of racism and sexism" (p. 140).

Sexism often is understood as it has been framed by White women, while racism is understood as framed by men of color. Both erase Black women, and neither captures their experiences.

Racial and ethnic categories themselves oversimplify identities and experiences. For example, Mahiri (2017) interviewed 20 people from multiracial backgrounds, showing how people shape their identities, choices, and practices "at the intersection of personal, social, material, and spiritual worlds" (p. 6). In the process, "prisms of racial identity" (p. 36) become prisons when they box people into categories that do not fit mixed and variegated lives. How, for example, do racial categories fit a family in which an Armenian American is married to a Chinese-Austrian American, and another Armenian who was raised in Lebanon is married to a Russian? In this case, Mahiri's interviewee described herself as "pretending to be white" (p. 49) because that is how others saw her, but she actually did not fit the limits of racial categorization.

Finally, the notion of multiplicity suggests considering how racial and ethnic groups interact with one another. While everyone needs grounding that begins from their own identity and social location, ethnic studies cannot create or reify ethnic silos. Multicultural education initially arose as educators and scholars from Black studies, Mexican American studies, American Indian studies, and Asian American studies joined forces. Similarly, today's ethnic studies should enable collaboration, intercultural dialogue, and solidarity across racial and ethnic boundaries.

Community Engagement

Since its inception, ethnic studies has been integral to activist movements for social justice across the nation. Because of this history, ethnic studies has been framed as an educational and political project, where curriculum and pedagogy stretch beyond the four walls of the classroom and into communities and other spaces.

Although currently taking place within classroom spaces, we see the clearest connection between ethnic studies and social activism in the proliferation of youth participatory action research (YPAR) and community-based pedagogies. YPAR involves students identifying social issues in their communities and using the tools of ethnic studies together with research to study up both oppression and social structures of inequality, while also using research to effectuate social change. And while YPAR is not synonymous with ethnic studies, attending to and nurturing organic and grassroots projects is at the heart of both fields. An example of YPAR in the context of ethnic studies includes semester-long units in which students develop conceptual tools for critically understanding how institutional racism has shaped their lives, bridging their renewed understanding to local issues (see Chapter 4). Another example is to equip students with tools, such as photovoice, that assist in telling stories (framed as counter-narratives) about themselves and their communities, thus challenging stereotypes, deficit narratives, and myopic readings of the conditions that encircle their lives.

Community-based pedagogies in the context of the ethnic studies classroom are rooted in community engagement and education. Community-based pedagogies rupture traditional models of curriculum development that distance classroom learning from the community rather than bring it closer. Because ethnic studies posits students as holistic beings and learning as a community praxis, grounding units of study in students' lived experiences and community ways of knowing challenges the notion that we can learn about race and how it intersects with class, for instance, without drawing from students' experiences as they navigate schooling and other institutions. Because students' lives and how they come to know the world are interwoven through their familial, community, and broader identity-forming institutions, it is important for ethnic studies to remain rooted in community knowledge.

But local or place-based knowledge cannot be used solely as a resource for critically reading texts and their worlds: Ethnic studies projects must engender critical consciousness that moves toward community praxis. Thus, community engagement may take different forms. It may occur at the individual level, where students come to a critical understanding of their lives as racialized beings; or at the classroom level, where students collectively work to understand who they are and how institutional forms of oppression deeply shape their lives; or at the community level, where students along with families and local communities take up education projects that inform, and often lead to resolving, key issues the communities face. Whether these projects materialize into local and national campaigns, the community-engagement dimension to ethnic studies is what makes these experiences come alive, as students (and their communities) are apprenticed into becoming advocates, social activists, organizers, and movement builders.

Pedagogy That Is Culturally Responsive and Culturally Mediated

Ethnic studies should transform how students—particularly students of color—are taught, but the significance of pedagogy often is overlooked. As an example, since 2005, the Philadelphia School District has mandated a full-year African American history course as a requirement for graduation. Professional development, while not required, is made available to teachers. Sanders (2009) studied how 20 social studies teachers (6 Black, 14 White) from various schools implemented the course; her results show the importance of pedagogy. Sanders interviewed the teachers about the course, its impact on students, and support they received from the district. Teachers said that the voluntary professional development they were offered consisted of content-oriented presentations by university professors and community/cultural excursions; pedagogy was not a focus. Only nine of the 20 teachers participated in it, and some were not aware that it was available. Sanders observed three of the more experienced teachers in the classroom for 1 week each. She found that all three were used to teaching as transmission of content, an approach they continued to use when teaching African American history. None of the three prompted much student interaction about African American history, and all three appeared to hold low academic expectations of their students. They struggled with disruptive student behavior, some using rigid teacher-centered instruction to manage it. Sanders concluded that teachers' knowing content did not mean knowing how to teach African American history to their students. We cite this case study not to critique Philadelphia's experience, but rather to show the importance of teaching ethnic studies through culturally responsive pedagogy.

The problem with enacting teaching as transmission is that the teacher does not focus on the students—who they are, what they bring to the classroom, what engages their interests and imaginations, and how the community cultural wealth (Yosso, 2005) or funds of knowledge (González, Moll, & Amanti, 2005) students bring might be leveraged to promote academic learning. Gay (2018) defines culturally responsive teaching as "using the cultural knowledge, prior experiences, frames of reference, and performance styles of ethnically diverse students to make learning encounters more relevant and effective for them" (p. 36). Alim and Paris (2017) emphasize that "our languages, literacies, histories, and cultural ways of being as people and communities of color are not pathological" (p. 2). A culturally responsive teacher becomes acquainted with students' cultural communities, backgrounds, literacies, and forms of expression, and figures out how to bridge these with abstract academic concepts in a way that both validates and stretches students intellectually.

But being responsive to students and drawing from their lived experience do not happen naturally. While it has become commonplace to think of learning environments as naturally leading to learning (think here of the student as a flower and of teaching, curriculum, etc., as the dirt, sun, and water), sociocultural theory helps us see learning spaces as rather complex, yet actively shaped by teachers (and students). From a sociocultural perspective, teachers need to be intentional with the ways in which they nurture these environments, paying particular attention to the spaces, tools, language, and any other cultural resources that mediate the learning of complex concepts, such as colonialism, capitalism, and heteropatriarchy. This active and intentional framing of teaching can challenge interpretations of teachers as "facilitators," interpretations that render them passive in the ongoing and generative design of learning contexts.

There is no singular way by which students come to internalize complex, yet abstract, concepts. Pedagogical praxis is an art and a science, and the educator as sociohistorical mediator (Díaz & Flores, 2001) understands how learning is experiential and always grounded in students' realities, and yet is attuned to the ways in which learning environments constantly are re-engineered and shaped by those realities. Díaz and Flores (2001) argue that "one of the most important roles of the teacher is to help create appropriate socioeducational contexts" (p. 34), teaching to students' potential and designing optimal forms of learning. Teachers as sociohistorical mediators thus ask questions like: "In and through what tools and resources do students come to know and transform their social worlds?" or "In what ways, and through what activities, are my students internalizing concepts at a deep level?"

Students as Intellectuals

Some people regard ethnic studies as "fun" and "cultural," questioning whether "real learning" happens in these spaces. Contrary to these misrepresentations, in ethnic studies classrooms respect for students' curiosity, thinking, and intellectualism has become a core value. Ethnic studies classrooms are ripe with students doing complex academic work. The notion of *students as intellectuals* represents a shift in the way teachers educate students, moving from deficit- to asset-based conceptions of teaching. Treating students as intellectuals entails a deep respect for students' experiences and their capacity to critically reflect and develop their own understanding of the world. Seeing students as intellectuals is, from a teaching standpoint, a disposition toward recognizing the intellectual beauty that students bring, especially those who come from the margins and whose marginalization remains a powerful resource for understanding cultural domination and power, and also how to transform these. Teachers who envision their students as intellectuals do not limit their learning to what standards define for them. Rather, they create, along with their students, educational experiences that enable students to "socially dream" (Freire, 2000) the world anew, but to do so with a rigorous and well-polished critical and reflexive understanding of their world.

From a student standpoint, treating students as intellectuals is a more accurate and situated understanding of what students do and who they are. Media culture, along with social media, has created master narratives about students of color and "urban" youth as dysfunctional, disengaged, and troubled. The same characterization and pattern follow with respect to children and youth who come from economically disenfranchised homes and communities. Yet what social scientists are excavating (see Espinoza & Vossoughi, 2014) are the rich histories of learning in family, community, and labor. People's survival necessitates a keen awareness of the world around them. It is this experience and intimacy with oppression that fuel students' desire to learn. But this desire must be rekindled through carefully designed learning experiences that bring such practices as critical literacy, historical analysis, and sociological thinking into the ethnic studies classroom.

OVERVIEW OF THIS BOOK

In Chapter 2, we review studies of textbooks and other forms of curriculum to show how the traditional curriculum is not ideologically neutral, but rather teaches a Eurocentric view of the world. We also review research showing how students of color react to this Eurocentric curriculum. In Chapter 3, we update and expand on Sleeter's (2011) review of research on the impact of ethnic studies on students of color, and on diverse student populations that include White students. Chapter 4 highlights several contemporary exemplars of ethnic studies curricula. While all of them are designed around core concepts in ethnic studies, and all of them exemplify several of the hallmarks of ethnic studies as outlined earlier, they vary widely in terms of scope, focus, and age level of students. Chapter 5 examines teachers' perspectives about teaching ethnic studies, based on interviews we conducted with nine ethnic studies teachers. Finally, Chapter 6 considers how research on K–12 ethnic studies can be conceptualized and conducted in ways that further both advocacy and program sustainability.

JOINING THE STRUGGLE FOR ETHNIC STUDIES

Along with the 1968 Third World Liberation Front and the fight to institutionalize ethnic studies programs in university spaces, we locate the institutional roots of ethnic studies in the Black struggle of the 1930s, the Civil Rights Movement of the 1950s and 1960s, and the 1970s turn toward multicultural education. We conclude this chapter by situating ourselves within that history, up to the present.

Christine

I grew up in Medford, Oregon, during the 1950s and early 1960s—not a place one would expect to produce a scholar and activist in ethnic studies. Medford at that time was almost all-White. In fact, although unknown to me at the time, the entire state of Oregon had been established as a White homeland during the mid-1800s (Brown, 2017). I went to school with other White students and was taught a White curriculum by White teachers. I have two early recollections of awareness of racism. When I was about 6, my mother mentioned that a meteorologist assigned to Medford was harassed to leave shortly after arriving because he and his family were Black. When I was about 10, while in the car visiting family in California, my aunt made disparaging comments about Black people as we passed them. When I told her she shouldn't put down people she didn't know, she rebuffed me. What I now find astounding is having just these two recollections of racism over a span of 18 years that included the Supreme Court decision *Brown v. Board of Education* (1954), the arrest of Rosa Parks (1955), the murder of Emmett Till (1955), the Student Nonviolent Coordinating Committee's establishment of Mississippi Freedom Schools (1964), and the many other events of the Civil Rights Movement.

I completed my undergraduate education in 1970 at Willamette University in Oregon, only vaguely aware of struggles to establish ethnic studies in higher education in California. Two years before I graduated, a coalition of students of color founded the Third World Liberation Front to attempt to institutionalize ethnic studies at San Francisco State University and the University of California, Berkeley; a year later, the first College of Ethnic Studies was established at San Francisco State University. Around the same time, Mexican American studies was instituted at California State University Los Angeles, along with Chicano studies and Pan African studies programs at California State University Northridge, and ethnic studies research centers at UCLA. For me, these were distant events that bubbled up into the news, then were forgotten. The Willamette student body was mostly White, the curriculum was White, and I didn't yet recognize the pervasive Whiteness of my identity and surroundings.

In 1971, I enrolled in a teacher education program based in inner-city Seattle, designed to prepare urban teachers. It was there that I came face-to-face for the first time with my own racial illiteracy. As an aspiring social studies teacher, I was placed in a racially diverse, working-class high school; White students were in the minority, although the great majority of teachers were White, as was the curriculum. Because the students were different from those I had known all my life, I began engaging in many informal conversations with them. When the program finished, I decided to stay in the inner city, although as a learning disabilities teacher because that was where the jobs were.

I gradually began forming personal relationships with a few teachers of color (primarily African American), and through conversations with them over time I began to learn how racism works. In addition, starting in around 1972 (the year the National Association for Ethnic Studies was founded, an organization of which I was unaware at the time), my racial illiteracy having become visible to me, I began what became a lifelong commitment to reading works in ethnic studies, starting with Ralph Ellison, Richard Wright, and Malcolm X, connecting what I was able to comprehend with the stories told by my students and friends of color.

I also participated in workshops conducted by Seattle Public Schools' Ethnic Cultural Heritage Program, designed to help teachers work in desegregated schools. The program's director, Mako Nakagawa, an educator who had been incarcerated along with other Japanese Americans during World War II, assembled a team to create a multicultural curriculum for elementary schools and to train teachers. It was she who first introduced me to the concept of multicultural education. James Banks's *Teaching Strategies for Ethnic Studies* (2008), first published in 1975, gave me my first direct encounter with ethnic studies. Although Banks is best known for his work in multicultural education, Black studies formed the roots of that work (as ethnic studies did for other multicultural education pioneers). I did not meet Banks for several years, but I took one of his courses at the University of Washington from his graduate student while he was on sabbatical.

For my PhD, I decided to focus on multicultural education, working with Carl Grant at the University of Wisconsin. After completing my PhD, I taught briefly at Ripon College, then in 1985 took a job at the University of Wisconsin–Parkside in one of the nation's first faculty positions dedicated to multicultural education. There, much of my grounding in ethnic studies solidified. I served as my campus representative to two statewide organizations: the Wisconsin State Human Relations Association, formed in 1979 to help teacher education programs prepare teachers in multicultural education, and the University of Wisconsin System Institute on Race and Ethnicity, formed in 1987, which held a wonderful annual conference and published a series of books about issues related to race and ethnicity. Similar institutes and centers focusing on ethnic studies, race, and ethnicity were being founded around the country, notably the Center for Studies of Ethnicity and Race in America at the University of Colorado, Boulder.

Around 1990, I helped to establish the University of Wisconsin–Parkside's Ethnic Studies Program. When my African American collaborator took a job elsewhere, I directed the program during its first year, then went back to teacher education. Because of these interconnected experiences, I have continued to see a strong symbiotic relationship between multicultural education and ethnic studies. In 1991, the National Association for Multicultural Education was founded—the same year the state of Illinois began requiring that Black history be integral to the public school curriculum, and 2 years before Berkeley Unified became the first school district to make ethnic studies a 9th-grade course and graduation requirement.

In 1995, I relocated to California State University Monterey Bay as a founding faculty member. The vision for the university, and much of the work during its early years, centered around building a multicultural, gender-equitable curriculum with an ethnic studies core. In 2005, I learned of the Mexican American/Raza Studies program in Tucson, Arizona, founded in 1998. I learned of that program when two of its leaders sought me out at a conference, then invited me to speak at the seventh annual Mexican American/Raza Studies Summer Institute. After that, I became an informal member of the program's *familia*. Five years later, the Arizona legislature passed a law (overturned in 2017) banning ethnic studies in the state.

Between 2010 and 2012, I served as president of the National Association for Multicultural Education (NAME). By then, nationally there was much activity directed toward diversifying the teacher workforce. This having become an interest of mine when my dean at the University of Wisconsin–Parkside created a certification program for teachers of color and I taught in it, I engaged NAME in figuring out what we could do; in 2012, we held a wonderful summer institute organized toward that purpose.

Because of my support for Tucson's ethnic studies program, I was only somewhat surprised when the National Education Association (NEA) contacted me in 2010 to request that I review the research on the impact of ethnic studies on students. (At first I wondered, Why me? Ethnic studies isn't my field of work. Then I realized that it had been for decades.) The report eventually would be used extensively to support efforts to institutionalize ethnic studies in schools (Sleeter, 2011). In 2014, El Rancho Unified School District in California passed an ethnic studies high school graduation requirement, which led to a wave of ethnic studies activism across California. The Ethnic Studies Now Coalition, a statewide advocacy group, was formed. School district after school district, including Los Angeles, San Francisco, and Sacramento, began adopting ethnic studies requirements, and in 2016 the state of California required the development of a model ethnic studies curriculum by 2020. Since my NEA report was being used to lobby for ethnic studies, I became involved in contacting school board members, writing op-eds, and speaking with news media about the overwhelming research support for the academic and social value of ethnic studies.

Miguel

I grew up in southeast Los Angeles from the 1970s to 1990s and am a child of the Chicano Power Movement, marked by student high school walkouts and the institutionalization of Chicano studies programs in university campuses across the U.S. Southwest. Southeast LA was then and continues to be a predominantly Mexican working-class community. Surrounded by industry and factories, it was no coincidence that my mother and father ended up as industrial workers. My father worked for 30 years as a mattress assembler and my mother continues to labor as a garment worker.

My commitment to culturally relevant education and ethnic studies was intimately shaped by my earlier schooling experiences. While I attended a bilingual elementary school, my experience with the dominant White culture was quite limited. I would characterize southeast LA as an ethnic enclave, which enabled close-knit family ties and fostered a sense of place. But what struck me the most were several experiences at the middle and high school levels. I recall doing a social studies report on the city of Bell, only to find how Mexican history and experience had been eradicated. While I didn't have the language and concepts to unpack how these master narratives perpetuated White settler colonialism, I always felt struck by the narrative that the "Bell family were the founders of our city." I recall stories at home about California being a part of Mexico and how Mexicans had been traveling to *El Norte* for hundreds of years. But somehow I could not reconcile how it was that an entire part of Los Angeles history was erased and rewritten as the city having been founded by White families. Later in my education, I experienced racial microaggressions. It was not uncommon to hear my White teachers say such things as, "If you don't study, well I guess you'll end up cleaning my trash," or visiting the San Onofre plant as part of a chemistry class field trip where the focus was on the kinds of janitorial and other jobs available to "students like you."

I would later reflect upon my schooling and come to understand that all the draconian and hurtful policies impacting working-class students of color, such as tracking, underfunded schools, a subtractive curriculum, and low expectations, were present in my own experience. It was as a response to this experience that I made the decision to become a teacher.

I taught English and social studies in my neighborhood middle school, the second largest in the United States, during the 1990s—at a time when a resurgent nativism and growing anti-immigrant sentiment propelled political leaders in California. I had the benefit of being mentored by amazing teachers of color and working under the leadership of a Chicana principal. Teaching and learning at Nimitz Middle School was a formative experience. Our classrooms were inundated with culturally relevant literature, written mostly by Black and Chicanx authors; our bilingual program was thriving, although diminished with the passage of Proposition 227, the English for the Children policy; and it was not uncommon for some of us to engage in discussions on critical pedagogy and the works of Paulo Freire and Antonia Darder. Operating in a prestandardization context (i.e., No Child Left Behind), we experienced extensive leeway with respect to the curriculum. I recall co-designing interdisciplinary units on environmental justice, where history and language arts came together with science and mathematics, as our students sought to investigate the sources of pollution in their community. While we didn't frame our work as youth participatory action research, these interdisciplinary units had all the critical elements of YPAR, drawing upon the strengths of community-based education.

My most formative years, however, came via continued mentorship and teaching in alternative education projects from 2002 to 2014. During 2002 to 2005, I was part of the Decolonizing Pedagogies Project. It was also a time when school districts were experimenting with ethnic studies courses; in 2005, some Philadelphia high schools made African American studies a graduation requirement and San Francisco Unified developed a pilot ethnic studies course. Led by Carlos Tejeda, who was one of the first to theorize and implement decolonizing pedagogical experiences for migrant farmworker youth, many of us learned firsthand the empowering aspects of Freirean and decolonizing pedagogies. Over the next 8 years I taught in other spaces, mostly summer programs, exploring ways that decolonizing pedagogies transform social studies and writing as fields.

I became an assistant professor of teacher education in 2010 when I joined the faculty at California State University Fullerton. Drawing upon my experience as a community organizer in south Los Angeles, I was intentional about joining others in creating spaces of support for social justice educators. It was at this stage that I joined the movement for ethnic studies in California. In 2011, precisely when the Mexican American/Raza Studies program was under attack in Arizona, I helped launch the California chapter of the National Association for Multicultural Education, which has now taken on a set of yearly conferences centered on ethnic studies teacher professional development. After relocating and joining the faculty at Chapman University, I worked with key organizers in putting together spaces for nurturing ethnic studies at the campus and in local Orange County school districts—spaces that have paralleled historic school district motions across the state of California, beginning in 2014 when El Rancho Unified adopted an ethnic studies graduation requirement course.

My commitment to ethnic studies has transpired via teacher education, both institutionally and in community spaces, as well as in the design of alternative educational spaces that serve Chicanx urban youth and migrant farmworker students. My own development has been generative and a space of learning. While I am not formally a student of ethnic studies in the traditional sense, my experience as a community organizer, teacher, and teacher educator have been integral to my conceptualization, pedagogical praxis, and advocacy for ethnic studies. My current work explores alternative, Indigenous/Meso-American epistemologies, and how these, together with decolonizing pedagogical frameworks, can seed transformative experiences and sustainable resources by and for Chicanx students and their families.

CHAPTER 2

Mainstream Curriculum as (Multicultural) White Studies

Several years ago, Christine was teaching a class of preservice teachers how to analyze textbooks to uncover whose point(s) of view they embodied. The class had been studying cultural diversity, institutional racism, and movements to challenge racism. She assigned her students to use an instrument she and Carl Grant had developed (Grant & Sleeter, 2009, pp. 128–134) to analyze one textbook currently used in schools, then bring their results to class for discussion.

Most of the students were surprised to discover how much the texts, none more than 10 years old, still marginalized people of color. One student blurted out, "This is White studies!" What they earlier had regarded as "just the curriculum" had been unmasked. When Christine asked why they thought textbooks continued to feature mainly White narratives while marginalizing those of communities of color, a student replied, "Because if we knew all this history, we'd get involved trying to change things." What was interesting was not just the student's growing awareness of curriculum as a form of social control, but also the fact that she was White, and she realized the damaging impact of a White studies curriculum, even on people like her.

We often hear comments that today's curriculum features diverse racial and ethnic groups. Textbooks are more diverse now than they were when many middle-aged educators were children, and state standards in history/social studies usually speak to diversity. Then why would there be a need for ethnic studies?

This chapter reviews research analyzing whose perspectives dominate K–12 curriculum materials. Apple (2004) explains that curriculum teaches a way of looking at the world—"the commonsense interpretations that we use" (p. 5)—including interpretations of the social system, of people like oneself, and of people we consider different from ourselves. Although people of color now appear overall, as we will show, curriculum still reflects White heterosexual male studies. In what follows, we delineate the major strategies, or narrative tropes, used in curriculum documents, particularly textbooks, to center White experiences while marginalizing and negating the experiences of people of color. We then review research on how students from various backgrounds—mainly students of color—think about the Whiteness of the curriculum.

WHOSE VIEWPOINT STRUCTURES CURRICULUM?
A CONTESTED DOMAIN

Because of the power of curriculum to instill conceptual lenses, and to draw attention to some phenomena while obscuring, distorting, or hiding others, curriculum often is contested. Central to struggles over what should be in the curriculum is the matter of who gets to define it, as a means for cultural and social control and the maintenance of power over others.

Although this chapter focuses mainly on textbooks, we situate textbooks within a larger view of curriculum that we use later in this book. Beyer and Liston (1996) defined curriculum as:

> the centerpiece of educational activity. It includes the formal, overt knowledge that is central to the activities of teaching, as well as more tacit, subliminal messages—transmitted through the process of acting and interacting within a particular kind of institution—that foster the inculcation of particular values, attitudes, and dispositions. (p. xv)

Curriculum functions as a kind of layered narrative. Overt messages and viewpoints are taught through a variety of multimodal texts, such as textbooks and other materials like novels, curriculum packages, videos, and online curriculum resources, and even classroom discourse. Classrooms also teach curriculum through less tangible but equally powerful venues, such as which students receive most and least teacher attention, or which students are academically challenged and which are not. Further, curriculum includes what students learn from one another through discussion, informal talk, and other interactions. Across these varied venues, the viewpoints present in the classroom may vary widely.

Nonetheless, teachers and texts generally structure classroom knowledge, at least at an official level, and this knowledge is what ethnic studies contests. Ethnic studies came about in opposition to overwhelmingly White curriculum narratives. Student movements of the late 1960s demanded curriculum from points of view of people of color, relevant to issues that communities of color face. These demands directly challenged curriculum's selective tradition in which some peoples' knowledge is taught while others' is not. As Luke (1991) explained:

> Curriculum always entails a selection from culture and from myriad possible literacies. . . . The literature we select, the methods and strategies we use to teach

and assess, and the knowledges and competencies we disburse selectively to different groups of students, are selections from the plurality of cultures extant in modern Western nation states. Perhaps more importantly, these selections are not random, but selections which serve particular economic interests and political ends. (p. 133)

Apple (2004) argued that the selective tradition "within the terms of an effective dominant culture, is always passed off as 'the tradition,' the significant past. But always the selectivity is the point; the way in which from a whole possible area of past and present, certain meanings and practices are chosen for emphasis, certain other meanings and practices are neglected and excluded" (p. 5). Apple explained that through the process of deciding which knowledge to teach to whom, schools "create and recreate forms of consciousness that enable social control to be maintained without the necessity of dominant groups having to resort to overt mechanisms of domination" (p. 2). When this process is unmasked, as in the example that opened this chapter, teachers often feel upset, although not necessarily equipped to work with alternative bodies of knowledge.

Many schools, especially those under pressure to raise student test scores, require teachers to adhere closely to the prescribed curriculum (Crocco & Costigan, 2007; Valli, Croninger, Chambliss, Graeber, & Buese, 2008). New teachers who are in the process of becoming familiar with their curriculum generally rely on textbooks (Grossman & Thompson, 2008; Kaufmann, Johnson, Kardos, Liu, & Peske, 2002). As teachers gain experience, many learn to adapt their use of texts, strategically selecting from them and supplementing them with other materials (Sosniak & Stodolsky, 1993).

But even when teachers do not have to adhere to textbook narratives, they usually participate in the same selective tradition as textbook publishers. Teacher-created curriculum reflects teachers' ideologies. About 80% of teachers in the United States are White, and the great majority (White and of color) have not taken ethnic studies courses. We find Vaught and Castagno's (2008) analysis of White teacher ideologies very insightful and suggestive of the ideologies that inform teacher-created curriculum. The authors drew on data from two studies of White teachers' experiences with professional development to address the achievement gap in different parts of the United States. Although the teachers varied in their understanding of race and racism, there were common patterns. The main commonality was that virtually all of them understood race in individual, rather than structural, systemic terms. Unaware of the structural racism of institutions (including schools) within which they lived and worked, they saw racism as an individual pathology most did not believe they had. Many rejected responsibility for the structurally produced achievement gap that they believed they were being asked to assume as individuals (although they were unaware of its structural nature). Even the teachers who recognized White privilege defined it in individual terms rather than in terms of collective use of power. Most of the teachers (and administrators) found culture a more comfortable concept to work with than race, although they tended to see culture as something people of color (but not White people) have. Many of them framed culture within a narrative of immigrant groups becoming culturally assimilated, a narrative that fit their own European immigrant family story.

This framing was similar to Picower's (2009) finding that White preservice teachers she studied used religion and White ethnicity as tropes to argue that everyone is different in some way; people of color should just pick themselves up by their bootstraps the way the preservice teachers' White ancestors did. Viewing racism as having been largely resolved, the teachers saw Whites as the victims of racial discrimination today.

These themes—individualism absent an analysis of systemic racism, inequalities as arising from cultural differences, and European immigrant cultural assimilation as a template to understand everyone—shape White versions of multicultural curriculum. Because of the Whiteness of the teaching profession, we venture to say that most teacher-created curriculum, even when including diverse groups, still represents an uncritical and White perspective, or what Berchini (2016) calls "inclusion for inclusion's sake."

Because of the importance of textbooks in shaping classroom curriculum, they have been the subject of content analysis for decades to determine which groups are included and excluded, how groups are portrayed, and whose point of view predominates. Beginning with school desegregation and the ethnic revival movement of the late 1960s, educators and scholars of color pressed schools, school districts, and textbook companies to produce and offer curricula that included their communities. Textbooks were the main focus of concern. As Gay (1983) noted, "Textbook analysts provided additional support to minority demands for an accurate depiction of their heritages and experiences in the school curriculum" (p. 561). During the 1970s and 1980s, it was common for textbook companies to hold conferences in which scholars presented their analyses of texts and recommended changes. Christine participated in several such conferences and consulting venues. In preparation for doing so, she and Carl Grant synthesized several textbook analysis instruments to develop their own (Grant & Sleeter, 2009), which can be used quite easily across subject areas. It relies largely on counting representation of people by race, gender, and disability.

Using the instrument, they analyzed 47 elementary textbooks published between 1980 and 1988 in social studies, reading/language arts, science, and mathematics (Sleeter & Grant, 1991). They found that the texts consistently gave the most attention to Whites, showing them in the widest variety of roles and giving them dominance over storylines and accomplishments. African Americans were represented more than earlier, but still in a limited range of roles and with only a sketchy account historically, mainly in relationship to slavery. Asian Americans and Latinxs* appeared only sporadically, receiving virtually no attention in history. American Indians, conversely, were depicted almost solely, but sporadically, in history texts. This analysis provides a good snapshot of textbook inclusion of diverse groups during the 1970s and 1980s.

While publishers made many additions to and substitutions from earlier texts, rarely did they actually rewrite texts or produce new ones.** Christine recalls realizing, during a visit to a textbook publishing company, that textbooks would continue to reflect mainly White perspectives. Like most other textbook publishers, this one held its texts to a production schedule that enabled small changes but not major revisions. Christine was taken into a production room where a staff of mainly White women (former teachers, she learned) was updating a text by editing content and photos. While the staff had input from consultants such as her, the fact that they were demographically similar to classroom teachers suggested that the viewpoint they brought to their work would not challenge viewpoints embedded in the texts. Later, the executive who had invited her commented that her observation about the texts supporting militarism would be ignored, of course, because "we are owned by Raytheon" (which manufactures missiles and other defense weaponry).

During the 1990s, national attention shifted away from equity and toward establishing curriculum standards and systems of accountability. As a result, with a few exceptions, efforts to continue diversifying representation and viewpoints in texts and other curriculum materials were muted by efforts to align textbooks with state standards.

WHAT DO CURRENT CURRICULUM ANALYSES FIND?

A simple method of analysis consists of counting people in images, people who are named for study, or main characters in stories, identifying each person by race and gender. In the process of counting, one also can attend to how each group is represented: what characteristics they have, the presence or absence of common stereotypes, and roles people occupy. Simply counting does not probe into the deeper narrative text structures, but it does provide a useful way of "taking the temperature" regarding whose perspectives dominate. A more complex method of analysis consists of comparing

---

*Here and throughout the book we use Latinx as a gender-inclusive term that represents the singular for Latino/a, and Latinxs to represent the plural. For consistency, and at the request of the publisher, we have used this gender-inclusive term. However, while the usage has become common among published scholarly work, and has been diffused throughout universities across the United States, we recognize complications with the use of the term *Latinx*.

**There were some exceptions, such as Globe Fearon's history and literature texts and Harcourt's *African American Literature* text.

the treatment of ideas, events, narratives, people, or movements in texts with those in ethnic studies intellectual literature. In other words, this method involves a critical reading of classroom texts through the lens of ethnic studies intellectual work.

In what follows, we synthesize research from both kinds of analysis, focusing on the United States. Similar kinds of textbook and other curricular analyses are conducted all over the world; however, since this book focuses on ethnic studies within the United States, we limited our synthesis of the research accordingly. After briefly describing a typology of curriculum transformation that we will use, we synthesize findings from analyses of curriculum standards and tests.

Banks's Analytical Framework

We will discuss the research synthesis that follows in relationship to Banks's (1999) highly useful differentiation of levels of inclusion of knowledge by historically marginalized groups in the curriculum. A *contributions approach* adds content largely limited to holidays and heroes, and an *additive approach* adds content, concepts, and themes to otherwise unreconstructed lessons, units, and courses of study. In both cases, inclusion is limited; the curriculum is not substantially broadened to include diverse perspectives. Conversely, a *transformative approach* to curriculum design "changes the canon, paradigms, and basic assumptions of the curriculum and enables students to view concepts, issues, themes, and problems from different perspectives and points of view" (p. 31). A *social action* approach extends the transformative approach by connecting knowledge to action, engaging students in action projects that address issues they have studied.

Curriculum Standards and Texts

While most of the research analyzes textbooks, there have been some analyses of state curriculum standards. Heilig, Brown, and Brown's (2012) analysis of the Texas social studies standards reveals a significant pattern: additions of more diverse peoples into the curriculum, while maintaining a White point of view. Heilig, Brown, and Brown found individuals or groups of color (the vast majority being African American) in about one-third of the standards. This might suggest progress toward transforming curriculum, until we look more deeply into how individuals and groups were added. The authors found that the addition of people and contributions ultimately did not transform the pervasive White narrative. For example, by using "such as" in the standards (e.g., students could study "social issues *such as* immigration" [p. 412]), teachers were invited to skip issues related to race and racism. The standards also obscured racism by using the term *race* but not *racism*, failing to mention race or racial categories in contexts where race mattered, privileging the myth of racial progress, and framing the U.S. government as an agent of racial progress.

Textbooks interact with curriculum standards; we know of one study that linked both. As part of an expert witness report for the court case *Martínez v. State of New Mexico*, Christine examined how textbooks used in school districts that were part of the lawsuit interfaced with the state's curriculum standards. She worked with several graduate students to analyze 10 reading/language arts and 10 social studies textbooks, using the Grant and Sleeter textbook analysis instrument (Abeita, Chacon Díaz, Oemig, & Sleeter, 2016). She situated the textbook analysis within an examination of curriculum content standards (Sleeter, 2016).

Table 2.1 juxtaposes demographics of public school students in New Mexico with their representation in the textbooks. As the table shows, almost two thirds of New Mexico's students are Latinx, although that category is fractured by race. In New Mexico, the widely used term *Hispano-American* emphasizes Spanish ancestry and de-emphasizes Mexican ancestry, marginalizing experiences and identities of many who, as Gómez (2007) points out, may be *legally* White but *viewed and treated* as non-White. One tenth of New Mexico's students are American Indian, representing several different tribes and pueblos. Only about one quarter of the students are White and not of Spanish descent. As Table 2.1 shows, White students saw people like themselves plentifully; students of color did not.

New Mexico's Assessment Frameworks (standards) for Reading and Writing gave teachers considerable latitude and encouragement for selecting curriculum that was culturally responsive to their students. However, the standards also highlighted culture as meaning "other countries" at least as often as meaning U.S. cultural diversity. For example, 6th-grade students were to learn to describe how characters' actions reflect their culture, respond to "historically or culturally significant works of literature," and "examine connections between cultures worldwide and American society."

Table 2.1. Student Demographics and Textbooks in New Mexico

	Latinx	White	American Indian	African American	Asian American
Student demographics	61%	24%	10%	2%	>1%
Reading/ language arts (10 texts)	1–12%	37–73%	0–13%	9–33%	1–13(?)%
Social studies (10 texts)	0–4%	41–80%	1–10%	2–28%	0–8%

Eleventh-graders were to read significant literary works "from around the world" that include "significant modern and pre-20th century works of American literature, as well as Hispanic and Native American literary works." Note that in both examples, whose literature is "American" is not problematized.

New Mexico's Social Studies Standards for grades K–4 enabled a multicultural curriculum reasonably well, for example, recognizing various cultural groups within New Mexico and treating tribal leaders and tribal government as significant. From 5th grade onward, however, the standards increasingly mirrored U.S. history and civics in conventional textbooks. They followed the east to west storyline that fits experiences of Europeans and Euro-Americans, and they emphasized conventional prominent events and people (such as presidents, Acts of Congress, wars), adding people of color along the way. What they did better than most other state standards was to include tribal governments.

Now let us turn to representation in the textbooks. In eight of the 10 reading/language arts texts, and nine of the 10 social studies texts, White Euro-Americans dominated. In all 10 social studies texts, Whites (especially men) were far more likely to be named than members of any other group. Across the 20 texts, White people appeared in a wide variety of roles such as political leader, soldier, lawyer, police officer, the ruling class, hero, conqueror, nation-builder, inventor, entrepreneur, business magnate, artist, writer, explorer, scientist, student, judge, and outlaw. Analyzers noted that Whites often were portrayed as "self-reliant" achievers, wearing suits, and wealthy. While White men predominated (especially in the social science texts), White women were depicted protesting for the right to vote and in roles such as teacher, cook, prostitute, writer, and child care worker. It is to this predominance of White people and White experiences that people of color were added.

African American representation varied widely across the texts, although African Americans were not a majority in any of them. Only a few African Americans (such as Martin Luther King Jr., and Harriet Tubman) were named. The portrayal of African Americans ranged from nonstereotypic (such as an African American teacher) to stereotypic (particularly athletes); they appeared in roles such as boxer, cowboy, slave (in most texts), basketball player, Buffalo Soldier, Revolutionary War soldier, and citizens fighting for rights.

Depiction of American Indians was minimal, with the exception of one 5th-grade text that featured a story about American Indians. They were depicted largely in the past or as engaged in traditional activities such as playing a drum, painting pottery, plastering mud on an adobe home, and dancing. A few specific famous people were mentioned (e.g., Geronimo, Chief Joseph). The few depictions from recent times featured the code talkers and American Indian struggles for rights. Several texts contained stereotypic and sometimes offensive material, such as a caption referring to an American Indian as a renegade and reference to Indians defending their land as "hostile."

Despite Mexican Americans/Hispanos (European "conquistadores") being the largest demographic category of students, their depiction was minimal in most texts. Analyzers noted that depictions appeared accurate although skewed to lower socioeconomic status. Hispanos (light-skinned) tended to appear as senators, soldiers, astronauts, and artists; darker-skinned Latinxs appeared in roles such as food server, field worker, labor union supporter, and police officer.

Finally, Asian Americans appeared sporadically in the texts (some analyzers counted Asians in Asia, such as a character in China, while others did not). Asian Americans appeared in roles such as modern-day kids, immigrants, migrant workers, English learners, participants in a science fair, and Japanese Americans being incarcerated during wartime.

Christine noted some features of the curriculum standards that, although limited, seemed promising but unsupported by the textbooks. Reading/language arts was the main subject area in which the standards made an effort to represent diverse cultural groups, although they directed teachers toward cultural themes rather than social justice themes, and toward global cultural diversity at least as much as U.S. cultural diversity. The social studies standards were quite traditional, with three exceptions: diverse representations of people in grades K–4, attention to tribal governments across the grade levels, and a course on New Mexico history that gave significant attention to American Indians and Hispanos. Teachers certainly could supplement the textbooks or use other materials. However, when Christine surveyed 1,275 teachers about their professional development, she learned that the great majority of it focused on the Common Core State Standards (CCSS) and testing, not on multicultural education or culturally responsive pedagogy.

Let us now turn to representation of African Americans, Latinxs, American Indians, and Arab Americans or Muslims in textbooks generally.

African Americans in Texts

Scholars agree that while African Americans are certainly more visible in textbooks now than earlier, African American intellectual thought is not. Based on their analysis of U.S. history and literature textbooks over time, Brown and Brown (2015) argue that "subtly, while these changes appear to reflect a more accurate panoply of African American racial representation, they exist alongside and helped to sustain a new racial formation of post-racialism—that is, race and racism no longer matter in the United States" (p. 120). Brown and Brown echo McNair's (2003) finding in an analysis of children's literature that more Black characters gradually were added, but within an increasingly color-blind narrative, especially in works by White authors. While texts include more significant events in African American history than earlier, they decontextualize these events from a larger historical narrative, rendering them as isolated episodes (Pelligrino, Mann, & Russell, 2013). Content that previously was absent is now present (such as depictions of racial violence directed against African Americans during slavery). But texts continue to disconnect racism in the past from racism today, and to frame perpetrators of racism as a few bad individuals rather than a system of oppression, and challenges to racism as actions of heroic individuals rather than organized struggle (Alridge, 2006; Brown & Brown, 2010).

Limitations of textbooks intersect with limitations in teachers' knowledge, which perpetuates marginalization of the experiences and knowledge of people of color in the curriculum, despite often-good intentions. For example, the Southern Poverty Law Center (2018) investigated how slavery currently is taught, by surveying U.S. high school seniors and social studies teachers, analyzing a selection of state content standards, and reviewing 10 popular U.S. history textbooks. Essentially, the researchers found that slavery is taught without a context—events appear, but absent a sustained narrative examining the institutionalization of racism in the United States. Slavery itself is conceptualized as a social flaw, nested within a story of progress that assumes the United States is able to name and overcome its flaws. Slavery is framed as solely a Southern institution, thus absolving the North. White supremacy rarely is mentioned, and slavery is disconnected from its ongoing reverberations. Paradoxically, much teaching about slavery focuses more on what White people were doing at the time than on what African Americans were enduring.

Similarly, King (2017) describes a study by the National Museum of African American History and Culture in which 527 teachers were surveyed, in-depth interviews were conducted with 72 teachers and five focus groups, and social studies standards from all 50 states plus the District of Columbia were analyzed. The study found that teachers believe Black history is important, and many work at infusing it, but on average devote only about 8–9% of class time in social studies to it. Textbook content is limited, and King suggests that teachers "lack content knowledge, time, and resources" (p. 15) to go beyond what is in the texts. As Hughes (2007) explains, as a result of continuing to minimize attention to racism and White complicity,

> students perceive racism as a tragedy of the past divorced from other historical issues . . . and the contemporary realities of power in American society. When textbook authors bury the history of American racism within a larger narrative of inevitable American progress, students perceive race relations as a linear trajectory of improvement rather than a messy and continual struggle over power that encompasses both progress and, in the case of the decades after Reconstruction, significant steps backward in terms of racial justice. (p. 203)

Latinxs in Texts

Latinxs have received far less attention than African Americans in textbook analyses. Noboa's (2005) analysis of three high school history texts found treatment of Latinxs better and more accurate than it had been in the past, but widely varying across texts. He estimated that only about 3% of texts' sentences dealt with Latinxs, an estimate similar to the findings of the New Mexico study summarized in Table 2.1. Noboa also found Puerto Ricans and Cubans even more invisible than Mexican Americans. Rojas's (2010) analysis of Latinx works in four high school literature texts found that while much more is included than in the past, texts feature the same few authors, position the literature as "multicultural" rather than American, and draw too much on stereotypes. In an analysis of six middle school math texts, Piatek-Jimenez, Madison, and Przybyla-Kucheck (2014) found Hispanics considerably under-represented in comparison with other groups.

American Indians in Texts

With regard to American Indians, Sanchez's (2007) analysis of 15 U.S. history texts found that while they generally feature more positive portrayals than prior to 1991, only three "do an acceptable job of depicting Native peoples within the scope of the American experience in a truthful, accurate, and objective manner" (p. 316). Stanton's (2014) analysis of five widely used history texts concurs, emphasizing the oversimplification of Native peoples and tendency to place them in passive roles historically. Reese (2007) notes that while American Indian websites recommend excellent children's books featuring Native peoples, most children's books featuring American Indians are either classics that portray Indians as savages, or bestsellers that "present Native peoples as romantic but tragic heroes" (p. 235), disconnected from specific tribes and accurate tribal perspectives. In their analysis of math texts, Piatek-Jimenez et al. (2014) found few Native American images, with none depicting Native Americans doing mathematics.

Arab Americans and Muslim Americans in Texts

Although Arab Americans are not uniformly Muslim, and Muslim Americans are not all of Arab descent, these two overlapping groups tend to be analyzed together. Eraqi (2015) analyzed five high school U.S. history texts for their inclusion and representation of Arab Americans and Muslim Americans. Essentially, she found almost no inclusion "until post-WWII chapters that dealt with conflict within the Arab or Muslim world, and emphasized the many stereotypes that already exist about these groups" (p. 77), particularly the terrorist stereotype. She found "little attempt to acknowledge the way Arab- and/or Muslim Americans are a part of America"

(p. 78). Saleem and Thomas (2011) analyzed 12 U.S. history texts for their representation of 9/11. They framed their findings as "propaganda making," in which the texts portrayed the cause as "foreign," and terrorists as "Islamic fundamentalists," ignoring or downplaying U.S. actions that fed conflict, terrorism as domestic as well as foreign, Islam as mostly peaceful, and many Americans as Muslim. Both studies found Arab Americans and Muslim Americans depicted as foreign rather than as American, and linked with the terrorist stereotype.

Conversely, the American Textbook Council (2003) argues that the way Islam has been included in texts is overly positive, rife with "apologetics and denial" (p. 69). These opposing conclusions illustrate how evaluations of a group's representation are bound up with the perspectives of the evaluators.

Textbook Analyses and Intersectionality

Most textbook analyses focus on either race or gender; few are intersectional. Social class intersects with race powerfully, but is rarely the focus of investigation in textbook analyses. Forest, Garrison, and Kimmel (2015) suggest reasons for this absence: the myth of the United States as classless, lack of a common definition of class, lack of clear physical markers of class, and class being a taboo topic of discussion.

Anyon's (1979) thorough analysis of the class ideology embedded in 17 U.S. history texts found them shaped in a way that serves the interests of those with wealth. A similar analysis of contemporary history textbooks through the lens of class is needed. Some studies have looked at representation of poverty in children's literature. Kelley and Darragh (2011) analyzed 58 children's books published in the United States. While they found that most characters living in poverty were represented complexly and realistically, there were gaps. Specifically, books gave more attention to urban than rural poverty; White characters in poverty were over-represented while Black and Latinx characters were under-represented and there were no American Indian characters; and the books emphasized individual actions rather than collective actions to address poverty.

Gender has long been a focus of textbook analysis, although most analyses do not also apply the lens of race. Progress has been made over the past 3 decades in representation of females overall, although males still appear more than females, even in basal readers. While females are depicted in both traditional and nontraditional roles, some textbooks develop nontraditional roles much more than others. Topics in textbooks, particularly in social studies, derive from male more than female experiences (Brugar, Halvorsen, & Hernandez, 2014; Chick, 2006; Olivio, 2012; White, Rumsey, & Stevens, 2016). The few studies of representation of girls or women of color find them greatly under-represented and stereotyped (Eigenberg & Park, 2016; Schocker & Woyshner, 2013).

Gay and lesbian people, usually ignored in textbook analyses and virtu-ally invisible in most textbooks (Hogben & Waterman, 1997), are beginning to appear, although in limited ways (Smolkin & Young, 2011). We were unable to locate a published textbook analysis that focused on LGBTQ+ people of color.

Analyses of Digital Resources

Digital curriculum resources are only beginning to be analyzed for represen-tation. Cherner and Fegely (2018) analyzed 42 iPad apps that were designed as instructional tools for topics related to diversity, equity, and multicultur-alism. The authors found that while the apps were designed to introduce diversity (many doing so through stories), they rarely went into depth. For example, many of the apps included characters of diverse races but provid-ed little information about the cultural contexts of the characters. White Western culture tended to be represented as the norm to which "others" were added. In addition, the apps entirely excluded some groups (such as American Indians) and rarely included others (such as Jews, Muslims, and Hindus).

Summary

Curriculum standards, mainstream textbooks, and digital resources that have been analyzed rarely get beyond the additive or contributions levels of Banks's (1999) typology. In none of the studies reviewed above were text-books or curriculum standards written from a perspective other than White. None reflected Banks's transformative or social action levels. People of col-or (particularly African Americans) were added into a White perspective, sometimes in fairly significant numbers, which may suggest to teachers who lack content knowledge in ethnic studies that their curriculum is at least at Banks's transformative level. But the overall framing of the curriculum is still White and, with respect to issues of race and racism, lacks criticality.

This is not to say that there are no texts and other curriculum resources from points of view other than the White majority. Such resources do exist, as we will show in Chapter 4. But curriculum resources written from White perspectives have power in a way that resources from perspectives of people of color lack. Jason Low (2013) asked several prominent leaders in mul-ticultural children's literature why publication of multicultural books for children has not increased over almost 2 decades. The responses included:

- Cuts to school library funds;
- Loss of independent bookstores (likely to carry works by authors of color) to mass market bookstores (less likely to do so);
- Perception that "multicultural books" are not for everyone;

- Gatekeepers in the publishing world (editors, agents, marketing) are predominantly White;
- White buyers bring racial stereotypes to what they purchase;
- Increased power of curriculum standards and textbooks that reduce teacher-created curriculum.

ASSUMPTIONS EMBEDDED WITHIN (MULTICULTURAL) WHITE STUDIES

Whether textbook-driven or teacher-created, we propose that a White studies curriculum takes for granted the following assumptions:

- Knowledge most universally worth knowing originated in Europe (or among Euro-Americans). Such knowledge, however, is marked as universal rather than as White. Quijano (2007) explains that historically the physical violence of European colonization was followed by "colonization of the imagination of the dominated" (p. 169), where Europeans repressed local memories and replaced them with their own, including a European way of thinking and seeing the world. Working within a worldview of dualisms, Europeans divided people into invented categories (such as races), ranking them hierarchically and linking human and cultural hierarchical development with genetics (Kivel, 2013; Mudimbe, 1988). Under this logic, which was tied directly to physical domination and appropriation of land and labor, Europeans defined themselves as most advanced and civilized. By replacing local languages, cultures, identities, and historical memories with European ways of thinking, Europe, and later Euro-North America, sought to convince those who had been colonized or enslaved to accept the social order and their subordinate position within it. White-perspective curricula only continue this process.
- Individuals rather than social institutions and organized groups are the focus of attention. This individualistic focus may highlight individual agency, but it obscures the social and institutional contexts in which individuals live. Thus, for example, students learn to see racism as an individual attribute rather than an institutionalized structure, or success as the result of hard work, without recognizing institutionalized factors that enable some individuals to become successful but thwart the successes of others.
- A narrative of progress is assumed, which holds that problems gradually are identified and solved, particularly problems related to inclusion of people within a diverse democracy. The assumption that history tells a story of gradual progress implies that history itself is not particularly important to study, since we constantly are

escaping from or moving beyond the past. The narrative of progress also suggests that we do not need to do anything to address injustices, since they will get worked out over time.

- Racism and colonization are tragic parts of the past. These terms appear very little in curriculum materials; the term White supremacy appears even less. As a result, students do not learn much about these huge concepts. Manifestations of racism or colonization, such as slavery, are firmly located in the past. Downplaying or ignoring racism, colonization, institutionalized poverty, patriarchy, and heterosexism, or locating them in the past, fits with the narrative of progress, implying that these problems have been resolved and no longer exist.
- White people (men especially) as the "real" Americans who built this country deserve homage and rightfully continue to lead. This assumption is not stated anywhere, but it is operationalized in the overwhelming attention to White people and White perspectives across the curriculum.

A curriculum can be considered (multicultural) White when the underpinnings are based on White perspectives and experiences, but people of color (events, information, actors) are added in without much context. It has the illusion of inclusivity without actually being inclusive; it is a form of "multicultural" inclusivity that does not critically interrogate White supremacy, institutional racism, and capitalist exploitation.

For instance, the 4th-grade California history state-adopted text, *Our California*, published by Pearson, does not represent immigrants and racialized groups in derogatory ways, as did pre-1960s texts. Nevertheless, there isn't a single instance of terms that describe how power and systems of oppression are maintained. "Immigrants faced challenges," "life was hard for many of these groups," and "diversity helped build our state" are used throughout, thus recognizing the plight of working-class immigrants throughout the history of California. But not enough context is provided to enable students to understand why people migrate, how that is tied to systems of economic exploitation, or how they often remain in segregated or economically disenfranchised situations. The text *Our California* renders these systems of oppression invisible by perpetuating a narrative of voluntary migration and progress.

The (multicultural) White studies curriculum becomes a form of "cherished knowledge," especially for White people, that renders questioning it emotionally difficult. Jupp (2017) defines cherished knowledge as "Whitestream subject area content and related whitened intellectual habits that form the basis of much mainstream learning and teaching in U.S. schools" (p. 17). The term *cherished* signals an emotional attachment that goes beyond knowing something intellectually and that connects that knowledge with one's own identity. Jupp introduces his own struggle by describing himself as

> a White middle class male from Texas and father of an interracial Latin@ family who spent 18 years as a classroom teacher working with predominantly indigenous, Mexican immigrant, Latin@ and African American students in inner-city public schools. . . . As teacher in racialised settings, much of my work centred on developing race-visible teaching that accounted for and advanced notions of race, class, culture, language and other differences in learning and teaching. (p. 16)

He recalls having learned the U.S. story of progress as involving conflicts between the North and South over slavery, agrarian versus industrialized societies, and states' rights. In that narrative, in which the North won, racism undergirding slavery gradually waned and popular uprisings (such as among factory workers, suffragettes, and civil rights activists) gradually extended and strengthened American democracy. But then he had to confront an opposing perspective: that racism continues to permeate both North and South, and that "White popular uprisings, rather than being foundational to American democracy, instead historically violate, defile and work against people of colour" (p. 24). In other words, social movements and uprisings of the working class, rather than advancing democracy, more often serve to bolster White supremacy. The crumbling of the lens he had relied on for understanding the United States—a belief in progress generally and racial progress specifically, coupled with a belief that working-class uprisings advance democracy—was painful. Jupp concludes that "cherished curriculum knowledge allows white preservice and in-service teachers to see their 'democratic' tradition as foundational to which people of colour might just 'join in', 'add to' or 'be welcomed into' though, in fact, elemental racial justice requires a different racial project altogether which critical race theories initiate" (p. 26).

STUDENTS' PERSPECTIVES

As explained in Chapter 1, a central purpose of ethnic studies is decolonization of students' minds—offering them narratives, analytical frameworks, and epistemologies that speak to the central concerns of their lives, from perspectives of people they are connected to.

Students usually are not asked what they think about what they are being taught, but they have much to say if asked. In what follows, we synthesize research on students' perspectives about race, racism, and curriculum. We organize much of this material by grade level, but since we located only one multigrade study of White students' perspectives, we begin there, as it serves as a contrast to the remainder of this chapter.

White Students' Perspectives Across the Grade Levels

Few studies specifically focus on how White students view curriculum through the lens of race. Epstein (2009) contrasted how White and African American students learned to view the United States in elementary, middle, and high school social studies classrooms. Overall, she found that White students adhered to "the progressive nature of national formation and development and positive view of national identity" (p. 76). As one White student put it, "Our country was put together by motivated people and people who wanted to change, to better themselves and our country" (p. 77). Several students expressed interest in learning more about contributions of communities of color, such as Native Americans. While the students viewed slavery as immoral and recognized other ways in which people had to struggle for freedom and rights, "most still had an optimistic view of national history and identity" (p. 76). About half of the older White students believed racism had been resolved, so when racial tensions rose, they blamed Black people.

Overall, the White students typically accepted what they were being taught about national history in general and race relations specifically. They didn't necessarily see what they had been taught as "White studies." Rather, what they learned inside and outside school meshed into a worldview they saw as more or less inclusive of diverse people and unproblematically true.

Students of Color in Elementary School

Interviews with students of color reveal strikingly different perspectives about the curriculum. These perspectives begin to emerge in elementary school, although most of the research into students' perspectives examines middle and high school students.

Many elementary school Black students interviewed by Epstein (2001) noticed discrepancies between points of view in the curriculum and what they learned at home. For example, although White 5th-graders believed the Bill of Rights gives rights to everyone, about half of the Black children pointed out that not everyone has rights. While Epstein found that both Black and White children learned (and later repeated) what their teachers taught them, by the end of the year the White children interpreted national symbols (such as the Constitution) as having granted rights, but none of the Black children did so. This contrast illustrates how students of color at elementary-grade levels are beginning to distrust what they are taught in school when it conflicts with what they learn outside school.

Students of Color in Middle School

Middle school students of color articulated frustrations with White studies curricula in several studies.

Two focused on African American middle school students. In Ford and Harris's (2000) interviews with 43 gifted Black students, they found all of them desiring to learn more about Black people in school; most agreed that this would make school more interesting, and almost half agreed that they got tired of learning about White people all the time. Similarly, in a study of a predominantly professional-class White middle school, Abu El-Haj (2006) found that the students of color (mainly African American) felt marginalized and "angry that African American history was rarely discussed outside Black History Month and was almost always portrayed in terms of victimization" (p. 154). Students posited that teachers avoided in-depth discussions of race and racism out of fear that the Black students would react violently. While a few teachers tried to infuse attention to multiple social groups into their curriculum, most students of color "framed their desire for a more representative curriculum in terms of learning about one's 'own' cultural history and literature" first, before going on to study other groups (p. 156).

Two studies focused on Latinx middle school students in history classes. Almarza and Fehn (1998) found that in an 8th-grade history class, the Mexican American students (who made up about one-third of the class) "desired a significant history—one that resonated with their own experiences as Americans or as Mexicans" (p. 205). The students felt caught in a bind. They wanted to reject the authoritative White narrative they were being taught that positioned them and their families outside history, and they desired a meaningful history that helped them understand their own lives. But they also needed to pass their class in order to progress through school. Busey and Russell (2017) found that the 12 Latinx students they interviewed (6 Puerto Rican, 6 of other Latinx ethnic backgrounds) described the social studies curriculum as culturally barren. All of them wanted much more attention to cultural diversity—their own backgrounds as well as those of others. As one student put it, "Kids like me, I want to learn about where I came from, how I started, and not only from the United States, but from our culture and every person's culture" (p. 10). The boredom students described was magnified by the rote memorization and direct instruction pedagogy their teacher used.

Outside school, Saleem and Thomas (2011) interviewed eight Muslim American students after they read passages relevant to 9/11 in history textbooks. The students rejected or questioned the credibility of the textbook accounts. One student, for example, explained that being Muslim meant following the Five Pillars of Islam and obeying Allah, and as far as the student knew, Allah did not say in the Quran that buildings should be blown up. The students were interested in a broader study of terrorism (which could include, for example, the Ku Klux Klan). But they rejected the simplistic equation in most of the texts between Muslims, "foreignness," and a terrorist attack.

Students of Color in High School

By the time they reach high school, many students of color not only are aware of a Euro-American bias in curriculum, but can describe it in some detail, and view it as contributing to their disengagement from school (Wiggan, 2007). We located 12 studies that are mostly but not exclusively related to the history curriculum.

Four studies examined how African American students perceive the high school curriculum, particularly in history. Epstein (2009) found that African American 11th-grade students brought a fairly sophisticated analysis of racism to their understanding of U.S. history. Although their perspectives varied, they interpreted its history in terms of systemic racism from which African Americans continue to struggle for emancipation rather than in terms of individual rights. Because their perspective was quite different from their White teacher's perspective, Epstein concluded that the students "learned to distrust the historical knowledge taught in schools and turned to family, community members, and black oriented texts" (p. 115) for their education.

In two interview studies, Woodson explored urban African American students' perspective about the history curriculum. Six students expressed what she called a "contentious relationship" with textbooks (Woodson, 2015). They displayed a "sense of suspicion toward textbooks, despite the fact that textbook accounts serve as the primary source of their historical knowledge" (p. 60). They believed textbook knowledge is important, if for no other reason than that they needed to learn it to graduate. Some students figured the text must be accurate; authors "can't just make a person up" (p. 61). But they also sensed that the texts were missing information, particularly about Black people. In another study, Woodson (2017) interviewed two African American students about the White master narrative they learned concerning the Civil Rights Movement. One of them, who believed White people should be the ones to solve racism, "was only able to envision racial struggle predicated on assimilation to dominant norms, White acceptance, and interracial alliances." The other believed the Civil Rights Movement had eradicated racism, but this left him with a deficit view of his own community. For both, the White narrative they learned was strikingly disempowering.

Thornhill (2016) asked 32 Black college students to reflect on their high school curriculum. He found that the nature of socialization they received at home affected how they viewed it. Seventeen had been socialized to think critically about race and racism; most of them challenged how Blacks were portrayed in their high school history curriculum, and resisted by doing outside research, talking with family, or challenging teachers and administrators. The 15 who had been socialized toward color-blindness appeared to lack the intellectual frameworks that would enable them to critique what they were taught.

These four studies illustrate Black students' desire for an understanding of U.S. history that enables them to comprehend how racism works and how it can be challenged. Most Black students either receive this kind of education outside school—they are the ones who can articulate what is wrong with curricula that present racism as a thing of the past, within a narrative of progress and White benevolence—or are left with what is taught in school. And as described earlier, what schools generally teach about racism gives students of color little to work with that dislodges self-blame for their own marginalization.

We located three studies of high school Latinx students' perspectives. Two studies were about curriculum in general. In a discussion with about 100 high school students who had walked out in protest of anti-immigrant legislation, Ochoa (2007) found that they wanted schools to teach more about "issues influencing their lives, including the histories and cultures of different racial/ethnic groups" (p. 199). Based on interviews with 35 Mexican American high school students, de los Rios (2013) found that while they were aware their experiences were marginalized in the mainstream curriculum, it was not until they took courses in Chicano/a/Latinx studies that they saw school as offering a place to work constructively through tensions and contradictions in their lives, and to give them intellectual tools to "negotiate political and social dilemmas" (p. 69) students of color confront.

The third study highlights the diversity among Latinxs. Terzian and Yaeger (2007) found that high-achieving high school students of Cuban descent rarely challenged the narrative of progress and U.S. exceptionalism. For the most part, that narrative meshed with their own perspectives, although they also expressed some interest in family histories, elders' knowledge, and cultural heritage. One factor the authors believe may be significant is that most Cuban Americans consider themselves White, rendering the White narrative fairly unproblematic.

We located four studies of high school Native American students' perspectives. Martinez (2010) interviewed 35 Native youth. They told her that they viewed most of the school curriculum as preparing them for postsecondary education, but found it limited in actually educating them. The students viewed an educated Indigenous person as one who is grounded in Indigenous knowledge and the person's tribal language; they did not see schools providing this kind of education. Students were also frustrated with the textbooks' stereotyped representation of Indigenous people and persistent White perspective. Jojola, Lee, and Alcántara (2011) and Lee and Quijada Cerecer (2010) reported similar findings from interviews with Native youth in New Mexico. Youth want an education that is challenging and relevant to their lives, but frequently do not receive that. When Native students have access to a Native American history and culture course, they flock to it, but most lack this access. In a 3-year ethnographic study, San Pedro (2018b) found that some of the Native American students deliberately rejected what their teacher taught about American history that essentially denied their existence. One of the students made the decision to fail the class rather than swallow a White interpretation of U.S. history.

Collectively, these studies of Native American high school students report young people as wanting an education that connects with their identities and rejecting schooling that renders them invisible or nonexistent.

We were able to locate just one study of Asian American students' perspectives about the curriculum. Choi, Lim, and An (2011) surveyed the perspectives toward social studies of 58 Korean immigrant students ranging from grades 5 through 12. A theme emerging from the data was students' frustration with the patriotic White American perspective, lack of information about Asian experiences, and glossing over of injustices, all of which students believed created a hostile learning environment for them.

CONCLUSION

Despite efforts to make textbooks and other curriculum documents and materials more reflective of the diversity of students in schools, analyses of curriculum standards and widely used textbooks find them to continue to be grounded in White studies to which people of color have been added. While White students often do not see this bias or find it problematic, students of color do, particularly with respect to history and social studies. While some students of color speak out or seek out alternative information, others simply lose interest in school. Students of color face a dilemma that White students do not face, however: in order to earn good grades, score well on tests, and ultimately graduate, they need to master knowledge that conflicts with narratives learned at home and that marginalizes people like themselves.

It should be no wonder, then, that students of color have been on the forefront of movements for ethnic studies. As students of color have become aware that there is an alternative, many have become actively engaged in advocating for it. In the next chapter, we examine how students fare when they have access to ethnic studies.

CHAPTER 3

What the Research Says About Ethnic Studies

Chicano, Nahuatl, Cubano, that's all me. I didn't grow with my biological father, who's Cuban. I grew up with my mom more than anything, single mother. . . . My mom, Mexican from Jalisco, ancestrally Nahuatl roots. . . . My own experience and so many of my peers around me is like, "Yeah we have to reconnect, because if not it's just erased." Within us, at least. That's part of why I connect to ethnic studies so much, because it's literally doing that within education.

—R. Tolteka Cuauhtin, December 23, 2018

Tolteka Cuauhtin, an ethnic studies teacher in Los Angeles, speaks to the need for an education that is rehumanizing, one that enables reclaiming identity and ancestral knowledge. His own elementary and secondary education did not provide these things; he sought them out, eventually by becoming an ethnic studies teacher. Cuauhtin's words point toward a potentially powerful positive impact of ethnic studies on students.

Conversely, we sometimes hear that students should learn the common curriculum that includes everyone before they focus on ethnic studies. This claim perceives the common curriculum as widely inclusive and as building cross-group understanding; some who make this claim perceive ethnic studies as divisive. For example, former Arizona state superintendent John Huppenthal vigorously opposed ethnic studies on the basis that, in his view, "framing historical events in racial terms 'to create a sense of solidarity' promotes groupthink and victimhood. It has a very toxic effect, and we think it's just not tolerable in an educational setting" (cited in Cesar, 2011).

What kind of impact on students does the research actually substantiate? This question was put to Christine by the National Education Association in 2010. Her research review addressing that question resulted in the publication *The Academic and Social Value of Ethnic Studies* (Sleeter, 2011). In this chapter, we update and expand on that review.

For this research review, we sought published studies and reviews of research that systematically document the impact of ethnic studies (including

Afrocentric education, Mexican American studies, and so forth) on U.S. students, pre-K through higher education. We analyzed everything we could find, regardless of whether results supported ethnic studies or not. (As you will see, very few studies did not find a positive impact on students.) For this chapter, we did not seek studies of ethnic studies teachers' development, or case studies of ethnic studies teaching and learning processes that did not also report outcome data. Rather, we focused on studies reporting data of the impact of ethnic studies on students.

This chapter is organized into two main sections that emerged from the nature of the research. The first section examines the academic and personal impact of ethnic studies on students of color. The second examines the impact of ethnic studies on the racial attitudes and racial understandings of diverse student groups that include White students.

ACADEMIC AND PERSONAL IMPACT ON STUDENTS OF COLOR

Ideally, the ethnic studies projects that have been researched would exemplify all seven hallmarks of ethnic studies discussed in Chapter 1. In practice, that is not the case. Ethnic studies is a developing field, an unfinished project. Some curriculum projects in this review exemplified all or most of the hallmarks, most often the creation of curriculum from perspectives of specific marginalized and/or colonized groups. After that, there is wide variation.

Researching the impact of ethnic studies on students poses a challenge in that the purposes of ethnic studies—eliminating racism, decolonizing students' minds, sustaining minoritized cultures—are expansive. How does one operationalize them for research? So researchers have landed on more measurable outcomes—achievement on tests (standardized or otherwise), retention rates, graduation rates, and scales for academic self-concept, academic engagement, and ethnic identity.

We organized this section of the chapter into four parts that differ on the basis of which hallmarks of ethnic studies the projects emphasized and which student outcomes (academic achievement or personal outcomes) the studies assessed. We begin with identity and sense of self, since other student outcomes, especially achievement, flow from students' understanding of themselves as capable and centered in who they are.

Ethnic Studies and Student Identity/Sense of Self

Students' sense of identity, particularly their ability to claim their ethnic identity and link it with an academic identity, is crucial. If students have been taught implicitly that people like themselves are incapable and unimportant, doing well in school has little meaning. Conversely, we know from research in social psychology that having a strong sense of ethnic identity and high racial awareness is linked with young people's mental health and achievement. Feeling secure in who one is and whom one is connected to provides the basis for doing other things.

For example, Chavous and colleagues (2003) found that Black high school students most likely to graduate and go on to college expressed high awareness of race and racism, and high regard for being Black, while those least likely to stay in school expressed low awareness of race and racism, and low personal regard for being Black. Altschul, Oyserman, and Bybee (2008) found that Latinx 8th-graders (ranging from recent to second- and third-generation immigrants) earning higher grades tended to have bicultural identities, while those earning lower grades identified either little or exclusively with their cultural origin. These kinds of findings by social psychologists underlie several projects designed to strengthen students' ethnic identity.

Several studies have focused mainly on the impact of ethnic studies on student ethnic identity and sense of self, foregrounding the importance of curriculum for reclaiming identity. Eight studies of six curriculum projects that range from small after-school programs to the whole-school curriculum are summarized in Table 3.1.

Lewis, Sullivan, and Bybee (2006) and Lewis et al. (2012) reported experimental studies of a 1-semester African American emancipatory class for urban middle school students. Project EXCEL, which met 3 times per week, taught African and African American history and culture, and African rituals and practices. It was designed to build communalism, student leadership and activism, and school–community partnerships. It included considerable attention to racism, oppression, discrimination, White privilege, Black empowerment, and self-reliance. In each study, the sample consisted of about 60 students, half in Project EXCEL and half in a life studies class. In Lewis, Sullivan, and Bybee's (2006) study, youth in the experimental curriculum scored higher than those in the control group on communal orientation, school connectedness, motivation to achieve, and overall social change involvement. But in the Lewis et al. (2012) study, there was a decrease in experimental students' ethnic identity, which was this second study's main outcome. The authors suggest that there may have been too much emphasis on racism and oppression, leading students to distance themselves psychologically from membership in a victimized group.

Two additional similar studies produced positive results. Thomas, Davidson, and McAdoo (2008) studied the impact of a school-based program for African American high school girls. The goals and nature of this 10-week program were similar to those of Project EXCEL: to nurture Black identity and a collectivist orientation, and to develop racism awareness and liberatory action. The program taught African American history and contemporary culture, weaving in African cultural values, Freire's

Table 3.1. Ethnic Studies Curriculum and Student Identity/Sense of Self

Author(s), date	Ethnic studies curriculum perspective	Research design	Level	Outcomes
Lewis, Sullivan, & Bybee, 2006	Project EXCEL, an African-centered, 1-semester class	Pre–post control group	8th grade	Communalism, achievement motivation
Lewis et al., 2012	Project EXCEL, an African-centered, 1-semester class	Pre–post control group	8th grade	Ethnic identity
Thomas et al., 2008	African American after-school program	Pre–post no control group	High school	Ethnic identity, sense of empowerment
Belgrave et al., 2000	Afrocentric extracurricular program	Pre–post control group	Ages 10–12	Ethnic identity, self-concept
Wiggan & Watson-Vandiver, 2017	Multicultural and African-centered school	Case study	High school	Academic achievement, critical thinking, identity
Halagao, 2004, 2010	*Pinoy Teach*: Filipino studies class	Interviews	Higher education	Critical thinking, identity, empowerment
Vasquez, 2005	Chicano literature course	Interviews	Higher education	Ethnic identity

critical consciousness, and holistic learning. For the study, a control group of matched students not participating in the program was constructed. On various measures of ethnic identity, racism awareness, and liberatory action, participants scored higher than nonparticipants. Belgrave, Chase-Vaughn, Gray, Addison, and Cherry (2000) studied the impact of a 4-month-long extracurricular program for middle school girls. Weekly meetings featured various activities such as a Rites of Separation Ceremony, an overnight retreat, and arts activities. These were all taught through an Afrocentric approach that included cultural practices and relationship-building. Using various measures of racial identity and self-concept, the authors found a positive impact on students in the experimental group as compared with the control group.

Wiggan and Watson-Vandiver (2017) conducted a case study of a high-performing school that served African American students and featured a curriculum centered on critical multiculturalism, anti-racism, and African-centered perspectives. Similar to Ginwright's (2000) study, this was a qualitative case study of a school attempting to link the curriculum with student outcomes. Data sources included interviews with teachers and students and observations in school. Results of the interviews confirmed that students valued the African-centered curriculum that linked them with their ancestors and instilled cultural empowerment in them. The authors concluded that this kind of education produced "organic intellectuals" (p. 16) who were able to critically examine the world around them as well as achieve academically.

Halagao (2004, 2010) examined the impact of *Pinoy Teach* on Filipino American college students. *Pinoy Teach* is a curriculum she co-developed that focuses on Philippine and Filipino American history and culture, using a problem-posing pedagogy that encourages students to think critically through multiple perspectives on history. It offers a different perspective about history than students learned before, and some of it is uncomfortable; the program helps students grapple with and think their way through diverse and conflicting perspectives, then consider what to do with their new knowledge. As part of the learning process, the college students mentor and teach what they are learning to younger students. Through a series of interviews, Halagao (2004) examined the curriculum's impact on six Filipino American college students at the end of the course. She found that since none of them had learned about their own ethnic history in school, they described *Pinoy Teach* as "filling in the blanks." Students also described collisions between their prior knowledge of Philippine history, learned mainly from their parents, and that in the curriculum, which critiqued Spanish, then U.S. colonization. The students expressed interest in learning about their own history in relationship to that of other groups. They moved from seeing other Filipinos through learned stereotypes to building a shared sense of community, and they developed a sense of confidence and empowerment to stand up to oppression and to work for their own communities. Several years later, Halagao (2010) reported a follow-up survey of 35 students who had participated in the program about 10 years earlier; 30 were Filipino American and five were Euro-American. Students reported that what remained with them was a "deeper love and appreciation of ethnic history, culture, identity, and community" (p. 505). The curriculum, through its process of decolonization, had helped them to develop a sense of empowerment and self-efficacy that persisted, as well as a life commitment to diversity and multiculturalism. They also developed ongoing activism in their work as teachers, in other professions, and/or through civic engagement where they lived.

Vasquez's (2005) case study of the responses of 18 college students to a Chicano literature course closely parallels Halagao's finding. All of the literary selections were authored by Chicana/os and dealt with topics such as immigration, migrant labor, poverty, and Catholicism. Eleven of the 18 students were Latinx. The Latinx students all said that they identified with the texts and that the texts filled in blanks in their understandings of their families' biographies. They reported developing a sense of community based on recognition of similar experiences and hardships. Realizing that there is an abundance of Chicano literature prompted feelings of ethnic and personal affirmation, confidence, empowerment, and finally occupying the place of "insider" in an academic institution. For one student, recognition that there is a strong Latin American culture strengthened his identification as American. The non-Latinxs found shared human issues in the texts to identify with; they had to wrestle with recognition of differences while also seeing cross-group human similarities, and because they lacked the authority of shared experiences with the authors and characters, they could not direct where discussions went.

In sum, all but one of the studies in this section found a positive link between ethnic studies programs that feature a curriculum designed and taught from the perspective of a historically marginalized group, and students' ethnic identity development and sense of empowerment. Criticality was a central feature of all of the curricula, and descriptions of all of the projects featured culturally mediated, or culturally responsive, pedagogy as central.

Ethnic Studies Curriculum and Student Achievement

Research investigating the academic impact of ethnic studies curriculum builds on earlier case studies showing increased engagement of children and youth when people of their own racial ethnic group are in the curriculum. For example, Copenhaver (2001) worked with and recorded African American elementary schoolchildren as they read and discussed *Malcolm X: A Fire*. She found that the children brought considerably more knowledge of the life of Malcolm X than their teachers (including her) were aware they had, and in groups composed of only African Americans they drew readily on their shared knowledge of African American media, civil rights leaders, and everyday racial issues to follow the plot, make connections, and interpret the story. In other words, the students became "smarter" in the classroom. Case studies such as these capture what teachers notice about student intellectual engagement when teaching ethnic studies.

But there are tensions between ethnic studies and academic achievement as measured by standardized tests, mirroring larger tensions that revolve around who has the power to define what schooling is for. While ethnic studies should challenge students academically, standardized tests arise from a paradigm that rank-orders students based on their mastery of a traditional curriculum, then blames students of color for their lower average performance. Tests also ignore outcomes that students' communities may value, such as cultural identity and respectful engagement with the community (McCarty & Lee, 2014). Beaulieu (2006), for example, points out that education for Native students should "serve the interests of specific tribal communities. That interest is first defined in terms of maintaining social and cultural continuity with the past while adapting to change" (p. 53). However, as Cabrera, Milam, Jaquette, and Marx (2014) argue, because standardized tests are part of the reality students must confront, and act as gatekeepers to further opportunities, test results are useful, even if they are not (nor should they be) the only way of assessing impact on students.

Fourteen studies investigated the academic impact of 11 ethnic studies programs or classes. Table 3.2 lists these studies in relationship to the curriculum project studied, the grade level of students, the research study design, and the nature of outcomes for which data were gathered. As Table 3.2 shows, most of these curriculum projects were intentionally designed through knowledge frameworks of peoples who have been marginalized by racism and/or colonization. All of them sought to engage students intellectually by connecting them with knowledge that originates from peoples with whom they are connected. We organized our discussion of these studies in relationship to the cultural group being served.

Dee and Penner (2017) evaluated the impact of San Francisco Unified School District's 9th-grade ethnic studies program, which serves a racially and ethnically diverse population (see Chapter 4 for a description of the program and curriculum). The curriculum is organized around six concepts that unpack the working of institutional racism. The program was piloted in five high schools, then 4 years later extended to all 19 high schools in the district. Using a regression discontinuity design, Dee and Penner (2017) evaluated the program's impact on five cohorts of 9th-grade students in three pilot high schools, using data on student GPA, attendance, and credits earned toward graduation. After controlling for several variables (such as students' entering GPA and measures of teacher effectiveness), their "results indicate that assignment to this course increased ninth-grade student attendance by 21 percentage points, GPA by 1.4 grade points, and credits earned by 23" (p. 217).

The impact of Mexican American Studies (MAS) in Tucson has been studied both by program participants (Cammarota & Romero, 2009) and by external researchers (Cabrera et al., 2014). Cabrera and colleagues compared graduation rates and achievement scores (using AIMS—the state's achievement tests) of 11th- and 12th-grade students who did, and did not, enroll in MAS courses, constructing a matched comparison group. They found that although students in MAS courses entered, on the average, with lower 9th- and 10th-grade GPA and achievement test scores than control students, by 12th grade they attained "significantly higher AIMS passing and graduation rates than their non-MAS peers" (p. 1106). Because this

Table 3.2. Ethnic Studies Curriculum and Student Achievement

Author(s), date	Ethnic studies curriculum perspective	Level	Research design	Outcomes
Dee & Penner, 2017	San Francisco Unified School District's 9th-grade course focusing on critical consciousness, self-love, and action	9th grade	Quasi-experimental	Grade point average (GPA), attendance, credits toward graduation
Cabrera et al., 2014	Tucson's Mexican American Studies program developed through Chicano and Indigenous epistemologies	High school	Quasi-experimental	Standardized skill tests, graduation rates
Cammarota & Romero, 2009	Tucson's Mexican American Studies Social Justice Education Project focusing on Chicano intellectual knowledge	High school	Pre–post no control group, interviews	Test scores, graduation rates, sense of empowerment
Kisker et al., 2012	Math in a Cultural Context, developed in collaboration with Yup'ik elders	2nd grade	Pre–post control group	Math achievement
Lipka et al., 2005	Math in a Cultural Context, developed in collaboration with Yup'ik elders	6th grade	Pre–post control group	Math achievement
McCarty & Lee, 2014	Native American Community Academy, developed with community collaboration	Middle, high school	Qualitative; pre–post no control group	Basic skills achievement

(continued)

Table 3.2. Ethnic Studies Curriculum and Student Achievement (continued)

Author(s), date	Ethnic studies curriculum perspective	Level	Research design	Outcomes
McCarty, 1993	Rough Rock English-Navajo Language Arts program	Elementary	Qualitative	Reading scores
Matthews & Smith, 1994	Culturally relevant science content consisting of biographies of American Indian scientists	4–8th grades	Pre–post control group	Science achievement, attitudes toward science and Native Americans
Green-Gibson & Collett, 2014	African American cultural infusion	3rd–6th grades	Causal-comparative	School Adequate Yearly Progress rating
Duncan, 2012	Afrocentric U.S. history course	8th grade	Quasi-experimental	Academic achievement, student self-efficacy
Rickford, 2001	Culturally relevant texts	Middle school	Post-interviews, no control group	Comprehension, higher-order thinking
Tyson, 2002	Multicultural literature in social studies, using Banks's transformative and social action curriculum levels	Middle school	Interviews, classroom observation	Use of text, knowledge of social issues
Ginwright, 2000, 2004	Afrocentric culture infused through curriculum and school as a whole	High school	Qualitative case study	Academic achievement, academic participation

finding seems counterintuitive, they tested it with a variety of statistical modeling and sampling strategies, all of which reached the same conclusion: MAS improved the achievement of mainly Mexican American students significantly more than the traditional curriculum, and the more courses students took, the stronger the impact on their achievement.

Several studies have examined the academic impact of different programs that aim to decolonize Indigenous education. Math in a Cultural Context (MCC) grew from collaboration between Alaska Yup'ik Native elders, teachers, and math educators to develop an elementary-level curriculum supplement for 2nd through 7th grades that connects Yup'ik culture and knowledge with the National Council of Teachers of Mathematics standards (www.uaf.edu/mcc/). The curriculum includes 10 modules. Its pedagogy supports traditional ways of communicating and learning, such as collaborative learning and cognitive apprenticeship. Lipka and colleagues (2005) compared 160 6th-grade Yup'ik students' math achievement after using the module "Building a Fish Rack: Investigations into Proof, Properties, Perimeter, and Area" with 98 similar students in classrooms that did not use MCC. They found that students in classrooms using the MCC curriculum made more progress toward the state mathematics standards than comparison students.

Kisker and colleagues (2012) conducted an experimental study in which 50 schools that enrolled large proportions of Native students were randomly assigned to either experimental or control conditions. The authors tested the impact of two modules on 2nd-graders' mathematics achievement. Since the schools had not used the curriculum previously, teachers in the experimental schools were trained to use it, and researchers video-recorded them. In the absence of a state achievement math test for 2nd grade, the researchers constructed pre- and posttests to closely resemble the math tests for later grades. They found the impact of the MCC curriculum "positive, statistically significant, and moderate to large in terms of effect sizes" (p. 100), with a positive impact on both Alaska Native and mixed-ethnic student groups. They also found that in the following semester students retained what they had learned.

McCarty and Lee (2014) report a case study of the Native American Community Academy (NACA) that serves middle and high school students in Albuquerque. About 95% of the students identify as Native American, representing about 60 Native nations. The school, founded in 2006, collaborates with Native communities to construct the program's curriculum and pedagogy. NACA teaches three Native languages (Navajo, Lakota, and Tiwa), along with protocols for using them. The curriculum, following a model of culturally sustaining education, integrates Native perspectives through English reading and writing, social studies, math, and science; teachers create respectful family-type relationships with students in the classroom (see Chapter 4). The overall vision of the school is decolonization by strengthening students' cultural identities and cultural knowledge, and by grounding them as Indian within Native community contexts. McCarty and Lee (2014) report that student achievement, even using dominant-society standards, has improved: Test scores of 8th-graders in 2011–2012 increased over the previous year by 21% in math, 20% in reading, and 9% in writing. Because of the school's ongoing success in closing achievement gaps between Native and non-Native students, there is now a network of NACA-inspired schools that draw on its model.

Earlier, McCarty (1993) had worked with and studied the Rough Rock English–Navajo Language Arts Program designed to develop biliteracy skills of K–6 students, the majority of whom spoke Navajo as their primary language. Because a written Navajo literacy curriculum did not exist, the teachers developed one that was in Navajo and relevant to the lives of the children, such as the thematic unit Wind, "an ever-present force at Rough Rock" (McCarty, 1993, p. 184). McCarty reports that after 4 years in the program, the students' achievement on locally developed measures of comprehending spoken English increased from 51% to 91%, and their scores on standardized reading tests rose steadily after the second year. Those who participated in the program for 3–5 years made the greatest gains.

Matthews and Smith (1994) used experimental research (pretest–posttest control group design) to study the impact of Native American science materials on Native students' attitudes toward science, attitudes toward Native people, and understanding of science concepts. The study investigated 4th-through 8th-graders in nine schools. The 10-week intervention included science content as well as biographies of 12 Native Americans using science in their daily lives (such as a silversmith or a water quality technician). The control group experienced just the science content. The experimental group made greater gains in achievement than the control group and developed more positive attitudes toward science and toward Native Americans.

Several studies have examined the academic impact of some version of African American curriculum on Black students. Green-Gibson and Collett (2014) utilized a causal-comparative research design to compare the achievement of students in grades 3–6 in two predominantly African American schools in Chicago, using 2009 Adequate Yearly Progress (AYP) reports as the main measure of achievement. The researchers used school documents to determine how culture was infused throughout the schools. One school used an African-centered approach to curriculum in all classrooms and infused African culture throughout the school; the other did not. The researchers found "a significant lower performance in third, fourth, fifth, and sixth grade students' AYP results in the school that does not infuse African culture . . . , as compared to students who attend the school that infuses African culture" (p. 35).

In a brief article, Duncan (2012) reported a quasi-experimental study of the impact of an Afrocentric* U.S. history curriculum on the self-efficacy, connection to the curriculum, and academic achievement of 217 8th-grade students, most of whom were African American, using New York State

---

*Some authors used the spelling Africentric while others used the spelling Afrocentric. We have used the spelling that the authors used.

social studies test data. She found a significant positive impact in all three areas.

Two qualitative case studies investigated the impact of culturally relevant literature on African American middle school students. In Rickford's (2001) study of 25 low-achieving students, culturally relevant texts (African American folktales and contemporary narratives) were coupled with emphasis on higher-order thinking. She found that the texts engaged the students, who could identify with themes such as struggle, perseverance, and family tensions, as well as with features in the texts such as African American vernacular. In assessing their comprehension, she found that the students excelled on the higher-order questions, but missed many lower-order questions. She concluded that familiarity with situations and people in stories increased students' motivation, and that even though they missed many lower-order questions, students were able to analyze and interpret the stories well. Framed through Banks's (1999) transformation and social action levels of curriculum, Tyson's (2002) case study examined the use, in a social studies class, of adolescent novels about social issues. Of the five novels, three were African American, one was multiethnic, and one was set in Japan; all featured characters addressing social issues such as working with neighbors to transform a vacant lot into a community garden. Tyson documented students' developing understanding of the complexities of social action, as well as their ability to use text to derive meaning; most of the students demonstrated growth in both areas over the semester.

In contrast to the rest of the research reviewed in this section, one study did not find a positive impact. Ginwright (2000, 2004) documented an initiative to transform a low-achieving urban high school that served mainly Black youth from low-income families. To formulate a plan, school district leaders consulted with several prominent African American scholars whose work focused on Afrocentric curriculum and pedagogy, who subsequently persuaded the district leaders to base reform in "African precepts, axioms, philosophy" (2004, p. 80) and to structure the curriculum around themes in African knowledge. Over the 5 years of the reform, academic indicators (enrollment, GPA, dropout rate, suspension rate, numbers of graduates, and higher education enrollment numbers) did not improve and in some areas worsened. Ginwright argued that the reform plan pitted two conceptions of Blackness against each other: that of middle-class Black reformers who connected African and African American knowledge systems with origins in Egypt, and low-income urban Black youth whose central concerns revolved around needs such as housing, employment, and health care, and whose identity was formed through urban youth cultural forms (such as hip-hop) and local experiences with racism and poverty. Ginwright argues that cultural identity is important, but that we need to attend to intersections between race, culture, and class. Because the Afrocentric reform plan ignored students' class-based needs and identity forms, students rejected it.

Ginwright's study calls into question the pervasive tendency to conceptualize culture in terms of racial origins, without considering the everyday culture young people experience in environments shaped by the intersection between race and class.

In sum, 12 of the 14 studies in this section found a positive impact on students' academic learning, as well as other student outcomes some studies attended to. While all 11 projects emphasized ethnic studies curriculum content designed and taught through perspectives of peoples marginalized by race and/or colonialism, most also were taught well. For example, the San Francisco Unified School District ethnic studies program includes teacher professional development as an important feature. As Beckham and Concordia (2019) explain, "We remain committed to the belief that anyone who honestly engages in developing themselves as a teacher of ethnic studies can become skilled at it" (p. 325) and that students will benefit as a result. In other words, ethnic studies curriculum matters greatly; pedagogy matters as well.

Ethnic Studies Curriculum Infused into Asset-Based Pedagogies

Thirteen studies investigated the academic impact of six projects that infused ethnic studies curriculum into asset-based pedagogies, connecting the hallmark of curriculum as counternarrative with that of culturally responsive pedagogy and cultural mediation. Table 3.3 lists these studies. López (2018) defines asset-based pedagogies as providing "a bridge that connects the dominant school culture to students' home and heritage culture, thus promoting academic achievement for historically marginalized students" (p. 9). Similarly, Lee (1995) posits that knowledge of language use "for the African American adolescent is often tacit," constituting a learning asset. But, "because the knowledge is tacit and has been applied only to community oral interactions, its applicability to other related problems of interpretation is limited" (p. 612). By infusing knowledge that is culturally familiar or culturally relevant to students, teachers who take a sociocultural approach to teaching and learning connect students' knowledge, including tacit knowledge, with new and unfamiliar academic knowledge.

While most research reviewed in this chapter assesses the impact of a particular program or set of practices, a body of work by López (2016, 2017, 2018; Sharif Matthews & López, 2018) seeks teaching practices that matter most to Latinx student achievement. Her studies use multiple regression analysis, path analysis, and/or hierarchical linear modeling to identify teacher-related factors that contribute to the achievement of Latinx students in elementary schools. The teacher-related factors include academic expectations, critical awareness (knowledge of historical and sociocultural oppression and how schools perpetuate racial power imbalances), cultural knowledge (knowledge of students' household funds of knowledge),

Table 3.3. Ethnic Studies Curriculum Infused into Asset-Based Pedagogies

Author(s), date	Program or focus of study	Level	Research design	Outcomes
López, 2016, 2017, 2018; Sharif Matthews & López, 2018	Asset-based pedagogy: academic expectations, critical awareness, cultural knowledge, cultural content integration, beliefs about/use of Spanish language in instruction	Grades 3–5	Correlation	Reading achievement, math achievement, ethnic identity, achievement identity
Lee, 1995, 2001, 2006, 2007	Cultural Modeling	High school	Pre–post control group	Literary analysis skills
Krater et al., 1994; Krater & Zeni, 1995	African American literature infused	Middle, high school	Pre–post no control group	Writing skills (various tests used over time)
Adjapong & Emdin, 2015	Hip-hop in science classroom	Middle school	Various qualitative	Understanding, enjoyment of science
Stone & Stewart, 2016	Critical Hip Hop Rhetoric Pedagogy	Higher education	Qualitative	Successful course completion
Hall & Martin, 2013	Critical Hip-Hop pedagogy	Higher education	Qualitative	Engagement, retention

cultural content integration (ability to integrate culturally relevant content into the curriculum), and beliefs about/use of Spanish language in instruction. Together, these dimensions constitute asset-based pedagogy.

López's research has involved Latinx students in grades 3–5. In a study of 568 Latinx students and their teachers, she found that "students with teachers who have high levels of both expectancy and critical awareness perform approximately ½ SD higher in student reading achievement over the course of one academic year" (2017, p. 13). In an earlier study of 244 Latinx students and their teachers, she found that "teachers' reported CRT [culturally responsive teaching] behaviors in terms of language and cultural knowledge (formative assessment) were both significantly and positively related to students' reading outcomes. For teachers reporting the highest level of each of the aforementioned dimensions, students' reading scores were associated with approximately 1 SD higher reading outcomes" (2016, pp. 27–28). In a study of 368 students and their teachers, Sharif Matthews and López (2018) found that teacher expectations alone were not enough; rather, student achievement in math was mediated by teachers' honoring of students' heritage language and integrating cultural content into the curriculum. In other words, the teachers who used asset-based pedagogy most consistently produced students with the highest average reading achievement.

Cultural Modeling (Lee, 1995, 2001, 2006, 2007) connects the language-reasoning skills of African American English speakers with the English curriculum. Lee (2006) explains that African American life affords young people a wealth of cultural scripts and contexts that can be used in the classroom to develop literary analysis strategies that students can then apply to unfamiliar texts. Speakers of African American English routinely interpret symbolism in rap and hip-hop, but do not necessarily apply it to the analysis of literature in school. Pedagogy that enables students to use their cultural frames of reference engages them immediately in much higher levels of cognition than is usually the case in a traditional classroom. Cultural Modeling moves from analysis of specific language data sets that students are familiar with and that draw on elements of Black cultural life, such as Black media or the Black church, to more general strategies of literary analysis and application to canonical literary works. Lee's research assessed the impact of Cultural Modeling, using tests in which students write an analysis of a short story they have not seen before. For example, in a quasi-experimental study in two low-achieving African American urban high schools, four English classes were taught using Cultural Modeling and two were taught traditionally. The experimental students' gain from pretest to posttest was more than twice that of the control group students (Lee, 1995). Lee's qualitative research documents that when Cultural Modeling is used, students gradually learn to direct discussions interpreting and analyzing texts (Lee, 2001, 2006), although traditional English achievement tests often do not capture this learning process (Lee, 2007).

In the Webster Groves Writing Project (Krater, Zeni, & Cason, 1994), 14 middle and high school English teachers worked to improve writing achievement of their African American students; the project was then extended to all students (Black and White) performing below grade level. The project developed several principles based on what was working. One important principle was use of various literary works by African American authors. Over time the teachers realized that they needed to "acknowledge [students'] culture—not just by incorporating their cultural heroes into the curriculum, but by weaving the threads of their culture into the tapestry of our classroom" (Krater & Zeni, 1995, p. 35). Acknowledging students' culture meant recognizing teachers' own implicit biases. A significant bias was toward students' dialect, a problem only when teachers focused on correcting grammar rather than on helping students communicate ideas. As students' ability to communicate ideas developed, they became more intentional about their own use of grammar. Over the years of the project's

existence, participating students made greater gains in writing than nonpar-
ticipating students on the local writing assessment, then later on the state
writing test (Gay, 2018).

Three studies examined of the use of Hip-Hop pedagogy: one in science
(Adjapong & Emdin, 2015) and two in historically Black university (HBU)
English classes (Hall & Martin, 2013; Stone & Stewart, 2016). Adjapong
and Emdin define Hip-Hop pedagogy "as a way of authentically and prac-
tically incorporating the creative elements of Hip-Hop into teaching, and
inviting students to have a connection with the content while meeting them
on their cultural turf by teaching to, and through their realities and experiences" (p. 67). Adjapong and Emdin investigated use of co-teaching and
call-response (two elements of Hip-Hop pedagogy) in 6th-grade science in
an urban school. Using qualitative research methods, the authors found that
Hip-Hop pedagogy engaged the students. Call-response memorization deep-
ened their science content knowledge, as did co-teaching what they were
learning to their peers. Stone and Stewart (2016) studied Critical Hip-Hop
Rhetoric Pedagogy in a writing course designed to increase the academic
success of first-generation, 1st-year students in an HBU. Among students
who attended class regularly, the authors found a decrease in the number
failing to complete the course, particularly its required assessments. Hall
and Martin (2013) used interviews with students to explore the impact of
three courses taught by an HBU English professor. They found that the use
of Hip-Hop pedagogy increased student engagement and willingness to participate; it also helped them connect with historical material being taught.

In sum, all of these studies found a positive relationship between the
achievement (or achievement-oriented behaviors) of minoritized students,
and teachers connecting academics with students' home and community
culture through a combination of curriculum content students could relate
to and culturally mediated/culturally responsive pedagogy. Conceptually,
we do not see a huge difference between the approaches to curriculum and
pedagogy in this set of studies compared with the previous set, except in
the emphasis given to content versus culturally mediated pedagogy. What is
significant is that all studies but one (Ginwright, 2000, 2004) demonstrated
a positive impact on the academic learning of minoritized students.

Culturally Responsive Teaching, Cultural Mediation, and Student Achievement

Much of the pedagogy used in ethnic studies embodies learning principles
articulated by sociocultural theory. A major contribution of sociocultural
approaches, the concept of cultural mediation, describes ways in which cultural tools and artifacts "mediate" learning. Within this framework meaningful learning is optimal when teaching strategies make use of and enrich
the sociocultural context in which learning takes place. With an emphasis

on learning as contextual social practice and a clear conceptualization of the formative role that cultural tools and resources play in learning (Cole, 1998; Rogoff, 2003), sociocultural theory points to the richness and complexity of cultural mediation that draws upon such aspects as discourse patterns, interactional routines, text structures, language-rich interactions, meta-communication, modeling, and so on. Culturally responsive teaching, therefore, is not a formulaic pedagogy defined by and limited to specific scaffolds. While culturally responsive teaching leverages the cultural resources that students bring to classroom settings—and thus conceptualizes students' cultural backgrounds as assets rather than deficits—sociocultural theory emphasizes the context-specific and nuanced ways in which cultural tools and resources are transformed into purposeful learning. Here we review six studies of three projects, summarized in Table 3.4.

Table 3.4. Culturally Responsive Teaching, Cultural Mediation, and Student Achievement

Author(s), date	Program or approach	Level	Research design	Outcomes
Au & Carroll, 1997	Kamehameha Elementary Education Program: literacy adapted to Hawaiian participation structures	Elementary	Classroom observation, writing portfolio audit	Writing skill achievement
Tharp & Gallimore, 1988	Kamehameha Elementary Education Program	Elementary	Posttest— control group	Reading achievement
Hilberg, Tharp, & DeGeest, 2000	Five Standards for Effective Pedagogy	8th grade	Pretest– posttest control group	Math achievement
Doherty et al., 2003	Five Standards for Effective Pedagogy	Elementary	Correlation	Reading achievement
Doherty & Hilberg, 2007	Five Standards for Effective Pedagogy	Elementary	Nonequivalent pretest— posttest control group	Reading achievement
Bailey & Boykin, 2001	Academic task variation (verve)	Grades 3–4	Correlation	Academic task performance, motivation

The Kamehameha Elementary Education Program (KEEP), designed to improve literacy achievement of Native Hawaiian students, grew from research on communication and participation structures in Native Hawaiian families and community settings (Au, 1980). Elementary teachers were trained to organize literacy instruction in ways that capitalized on Native Hawaiian culture and interaction patterns, such as using "talk story." Over time, the project added additional features, like student ownership over literacy and a constructivist approach to teaching. Much of the research on the program's impact appears in unpublished technical reports, but there are some published studies. Au and Carroll (1997) reported a study of the program's impact on writing in classrooms of 26 experienced and skilled teachers. After the first year, using program-developed writing assessment, they found that students moved from 60% below grade level and 40% at grade level, to 32% below and 68% above grade level. Tharp and Gallimore (1988) compared the reading achievement in KEEP classrooms with achievement in traditional classrooms. They found huge and consistent achievement differences. For example, while the average reading achievement of 1st-graders was above the 50th percentile in KEEP classrooms, it hovered around the 37th percentile in traditional classrooms. Students in KEEP classrooms were also more academically engaged, and their teachers gave them far more positive academic feedback and less negative behavioral feedback than students in traditional classrooms.

The Five Standards for Effective Pedagogy, built on the KEEP model, grew from research on sociocultural pedagogical practices that improve student academic achievement in elementary classrooms serving culturally and linguistically diverse students. The standards include: (1) facilitating learning through "joint productive activity," or conversations with students about their work; (2) developing language and literacy across the curriculum; (3) connecting new information with what students already know from home and community contexts; (4) promoting complex thinking; and (5) teaching through dialogue. Research studies (many of which are in technical reports rather than journal articles) find improved student achievement when teachers use these standards.

In a small experimental study involving two classes of 8th-grade Native American students, Hilberg, Tharp, and DeGeest (2000) found that the experimental group, taught by a teacher using collaborative pedagogy to create meaningful products in an environment of content-rich dialogue, enjoyed mathematics more and achieved at a higher level than students taught through traditional pedagogy, although the achievement results were not statistically significant. Doherty, Hilberg, Pinal, and Tharp (2003) studied the relationship between 15 elementary teachers' use of the standards and reading achievement gains (measured on the Stanford Achievement Test) of mainly low-socioeconomic Latinx students, many of whom were designated English language learners. They found that the more teachers used the five standards, the greater the gains. Further, "students of teachers who had transformed both their pedagogy and classroom organization had significantly greater overall achievement gains in comprehension, reading, spelling, and vocabulary than students of teachers who had not similarly transformed their teaching" (p. 18). Similarly, in a carefully designed nonequivalent pretest–posttest control group study involving two elementary schools (one experimental, the other control), Doherty and Hilberg (2007) found that as teachers' use of the five standards increased, the reading achievement of their predominantly low-income Latinx students increased, although gains were small. Students in classrooms in which teachers used the five standards along with supportive classroom organization made the greatest achievement gains; gains were most pronounced for low-English-proficient students.

Following a different chain of inquiry, Bailey and Boykin (2001), in an effort to identify classroom practices that appeal to African American students, studied the relationship between academic task variation and student academic learning. Academic task variation refers to the variety of stimulation children are afforded in instructional activities. The authors wanted to address the boredom African American children often experience in school compared with the stimulation ("verve," in Boykin's terminology) they are used to in their homes and communities. Using an experimental research design in which children participated in a task of either low or high variability, they found that the children's academic performance was much higher when they were taught in a manner using high task variability.

In sum, all six of these studies find that conceptualizing teaching as cultural mediation, shaping teaching processes around students' cultural learning processes, engages students and leads to higher achievement. While the three projects did not take up the matter of whose culture shapes the curriculum itself, we included these studies because they highlight ways in which cultural artifacts, such as discourse patterns, collaborative and joint meaning-making, and task variation, mediate rich learning experiences that draw from a sociocultural environment that stretches from school to home and community settings. Including studies that emphasize sociocultural contexts in a review of the impact of ethnic studies broadens our understanding of how cultural resources function as purposeful and effective tools for learning, pointing to cultural mediation and learning processes that often can be overlooked.

ETHNIC STUDIES FOR DIVERSE GROUPS
THAT INCLUDE WHITE STUDENTS

What does it mean to include White students in ethnic studies, and what do White students gain? Some fear that ethnic studies foments racial antagonism. While White students are not the center of ethnic studies curricula, it is important to consider how White students experience such curricula. Here, we review research on the impact of ethnic studies designed for diverse groups that include White students. Most of that research has investigated its impact on students' racial attitudes and knowledge about race. We organized this section by general age level of students, since that follows how the research usually is framed.

Early Childhood Level

At the early childhood level (age 8 and younger), Aboud and colleagues' research review is very helpful (Aboud, Tredoux, Tropp, Brown, Niens, Noor, & Una Global Evaluation Group, 2012). The authors reviewed 32 experimental studies located in various countries (such as Ireland, South Africa, and the United States); 14 reported the impact of cross-group contact, and 18, the impact of instruction. Studies of cross-group contact tended to use peer relations as the main outcome, while studies of instruction tended to look at changes in attitudes. Overall, the authors found that 60% of the effects were positive, only 10% were negative, and the rest showed no statistically significant change. Sixty-seven percent of the outcomes for majority-group children were positive; most of the outcomes for minority-group children were not statistically significant one way or the other. Studies found instruction about racial diversity to have a more positive impact than direct contact with children who differed from themselves, although both generally produced a positive impact. The authors identified three types of instructional interventions: stories in which children identify with a character of their own racial or ethnic group who has friends from another group, stories exclusively about members of a different racial or ethnic group, and anti-bias instruction that focuses on how one might respond to prejudice and exclusion. Least effective were stories or lessons that featured another racial or ethnic group.

Studies by Aboud and Fenwick (1999) and by Bigler and colleagues (Bigler, 1999; Bigler, Brown, & Markell, 2001; Hughes, Bigler, & Levy, 2007) elaborate on the nature of instruction that has an impact on attitudes, especially among White children. This research supports the research noted above regarding most and least impactful interventions. Simply infusing representation of racially and ethnically diverse people into the curriculum has only a marginal impact on students' attitudes. Bigler (1999) explained that since racial attitudes are acquired actively rather than passively, curricula that simply depict or label groups or group members (for example, pointing out a person's race, ethnicity, or gender) may draw students' attention to group markers and differences, inviting stereotyping without engaging students in questioning their own thinking. What is more effective is to focus explicitly on stereotyping and bias, present strong counter-stereotypic models, and engage students in thinking about multiple features of individuals (such as race and occupation), within-group differences, and cross-group similarities.

For example, Hughes Bigler, and Levy (2007) documented the impact on African American and White elementary children of a few short lessons that included information about Black and White historical figures and (in the treatment condition) about racism. They found that lessons teaching about racism, and about successful challenges to it, improved racial attitudes among White children, allowing them to see how racism affects everybody and offering them a vision for addressing it. The authors posited that children's value for fairness accounts for much of the positive impact. Lessons about racism had less impact on the African American children (probably because they duplicated what they already knew), but the information about historical figures improved their regard for African Americans.

Using a pretest–posttest design, Aboud and Fenwick (1999) investigated two curricular inventions designed to help elementary children talk about race. They found that talk that reduces prejudice, especially among high-prejudiced children: directs attention toward individual qualities rather than group membership only; offers positive information about a group; and directly addresses a listener's concerns. Such talk is more effective than general talk about race that does none of these.

What this research on young children reveals is that positive racial attitudes can be developed best by directly confronting children's actual questions and assumptions about race, racism, and differences they see among people. It is also helpful to draw young children's attention to the complexity of individuals, as well as to examples of people like themselves who challenge racial discrimination. Interracial contact is not unhelpful, but by itself may not improve attitudes. The kind of teaching that impacts students' racial attitudes at the early childhood level is what provides a basis for ethnic studies at the elementary and secondary levels.

Elementary and Secondary Levels

At the elementary and secondary levels, there is surprisingly little research. Okoye-Johnson's (2011) review is useful, although the reviewed studies were not as strong methodologically as those reviewed by Aboud and colleagues (2012). Okoye-Johnson conducted a statistical meta-analysis of 30 studies that compared the impact of a traditional curriculum, versus a multicultural curriculum or extracurricular intervention, on racial attitudes of pre-K–12 students. The 21 studies of the impact of a multicultural curriculum that was part of the regular instructional program reported an effect size of 0.645, meaning that exposure to it "brought about more positive changes in students' racial attitudes than did exposure to traditional instruction" (p. 1263). Studies of the impact of extracurricular cross-cultural interventions (outside the regular instructional program) reported a much smaller positive effect size (0.08), suggesting that multicultural curriculum that is part of the school's regular programming has a considerably more powerful positive impact on students' racial attitudes than extracurricular cultural programming or no direct attention to multiculturalism, race, or ethnicity.

Two additional studies investigated the impact of curriculum on student attitudes at the high school level. Klepper (2014) studied the impact of his own social studies course about Islam and Muslims on the attitudes of 64 female students in a Catholic high school. He designed the course to provide historic and cultural background and to engage students in writing projects that asked them to think critically about their own assumptions about issues such as jihad and Muslim women. He found that by the end of the semester, students' thinking was more nuanced and for the most part their attitudes were more positive.

San Pedro (2018a) described how a White high school student changed during a semester-long course in Native American literature. He points out that by centering Indigenous perspectives and decentering the Whiteness that traditional schooling reinforces and renders invisible to White students, the course radically disrupted the White student's point of view. Initially she felt as though she needed to defend her race, which she turned to social media to do. But through the teacher's gentle affirmation of all the students' questions and sense-making, gentle prodding of students' thinking, and use of Humanizing Through Storying (San Pedro & Kinloch, 2017), the White student came to reconceptualize her identity and knowledge in a way that took "into consideration the lives, knowledges, and perspectives of others" (San Pedro, 2018a, p. 1224).

Higher Education

Much of the extensive higher education research examines development of democracy outcomes among students. Gurin, Dey, Gurin, and Hurtado (2003) defined these as including "commitment to promoting racial understanding, perspective taking, sense of commonality in values with students from different racial/ethnic backgrounds, agreement that diversity and democracy can be congenial, involvement in political affairs and community service during college as well as commitment to civic affairs after college" (p. 25). Research examines the impact of various diversity experiences, with a focus on course-taking and interracial interaction. For the most part, the courses in these studies are required diversity courses, lists of which include ethnic studies, women's studies, and general diversity courses.

The overwhelming and most consistent finding is that in most studies such courses have a positive impact on students (Denson, 2009; Gurin, Dey, Hurtado, & Gurin, 2002; Lopez, 2004; Martin, 2010). Engberg's (2004) review of 73 studies of the impact of a diversity course, a diversity workshop, a peer-facilitated invention, or a service intervention found that 52 of the studies reported positive gains, 14 reported mixed gains, and only seven reported no change. Although most studies had methodological weaknesses (such as use of convenience samples and limitations stemming from wording of some of the survey questions), there was still a consistent pattern of finding a positive impact of diversity coursework on reducing students' biases.

The impact of such courses is considerably stronger when they include cross-group interaction (Antonio, Chang, Hakuta, Kenny, Levin, & Milem, 2004; Bowman, 2010a; Chang, 2002; Denson, 2009; Gurin et al., 2002; Lopez, 2004), or, as Nagda, Kim, and Truelove (2004) put it, "enlightenment and encounter." Because of the importance of cross-group interaction, some research focuses specifically on its nature. Gurin and Nagda (2006) found that participation in structured intergroup dialogues

> fosters active thinking about causes of social behavior and knowledge of institutional and other structural features of society that produce and maintain group-based inequalities, . . . increases perception of both commonalities and differences between and within groups and helps students to normalize conflict and build skills to work with conflicts, . . . [and] enhances interest in political issues and develops a sense of citizenship through college and community activities. (p. 22)

Required diversity courses generally have a greater positive impact on White students' racial attitudes than on those of students of color (Bowman, 2010b; Denson, 2009; Engberg, 2004; Lopez, 2004), probably because exposure to a systematic analysis of power is newer to White students than to students of color, and because while most students of color have engaged in cross-racial interaction previously, a large proportion of White students have not.

A growing body of research examines the impact of ethnic studies, Critical Whiteness studies, or other diversity courses on White students. Several studies use the Psychosocial Costs of Racism to Whites Scale (Spainerman & Heppner, 2004), which examines three kinds of impact: (1) White empathic reactions toward racism, (2) White guilt, and (3) White fear of others. For example, Paone, Malott, and Barr (2015) found that a Whiteness studies course produced significant positive changes among 121 White students, although there were some nuances such as increased levels of White guilt and no overall changes in levels of empathy. In a survey study of 270 White students, Todd, Spanierman, and Poteat (2011) found that empathy, guilt, and fear changed differently through coursework and were moderated by color-blind attitudes students brought. While guilt tended to rise with exposure to information about racism, guilt often prompted White students to engage in more learning; the authors noted that too little guidance is available for helping White students deal with guilt. Students who brought a high level of racial awareness didn't experience a rise in racial fear, while those who ascribed to color-blindness initially did so. Neville, Poteat, Lewis, and Spanierman (2014), in a 4-year longitudinal study of 845 White undergraduate students, found that participation in university diversity experiences, such as courses and having close friendships with Black peers, reduced the likelihood of their saying they were "color-blind," and that the more diversity courses White students took, the greater their racial awareness. Overall, the research finds that diversity courses help White students, but not in linear or uniform ways.

For many students—particularly White students—the first diversity course is emotionally challenging (Hogan & Mallott, 2005). In a large survey study of students in 19 colleges and universities, Bowman (2010b) examined the impact of taking one or more diversity courses on students' well-being and comfort with and appreciation of differences. He found that many students who took a single diversity course experienced a reduced sense of well-being due to having to grapple with issues they had not been exposed to before. However, students who took more than one diversity course experienced significant gains, with gains being greatest for White male students from economically privileged backgrounds (who had the farthest to go).

CONCLUSION

We have framed ethnic studies as an anti-racist, decolonial project that seeks to rehumanize education for students of color, center subjugated knowledge narratives and ancestral knowledge, and build solidarity across racial and ethnic differences for the purpose of working toward social justice. This vision goes beyond the nuts and bolts that are visible in most ethnic studies projects, but it is a vision that is consistent with most of them. The research on the impact of ethnic studies on students, while limited in terms of research outcomes and (in many cases) the ethnic studies hallmarks of the projects themselves, lends strong support to the positive value of ethnic studies for all students—students of color as well as White students.

As noted throughout this chapter, almost all projects that were researched gave serious attention to offering curriculum that is grounded in perspectives of specific racially marginalized groups. While some undoubtedly did this better and in more depth than others, attending to the perspective of curricular knowledge is what makes curriculum an ethnic studies curriculum. Attention to culturally responsive pedagogy and cultural mediation was also a common feature of project descriptions. Some projects, such as KEEP (Au & Carroll, 1997), focused on doing this well, and some, such as the Mexican American Studies Social Justice Education Project (Cammarota & Romero, 2009), developed their own frameworks for what such pedagogy looks like. We suspect that the consistently positive impact of ethnic studies projects results from an interaction between what is being taught and how students are being engaged as learners.

The other five hallmarks received less direct and consistent attention in the program descriptions. Attention to criticality, while visible to some extent in most project descriptions, varied. For example, while Halagao (2004) explained that the critical perspective in *Pinoy Teach* was difficult initially for some students, Math in a Cultural Context (Lipka et al., 2005), which connects math with Yup'ik everyday culture, did not appear to employ criticality. Does every ethnic studies project need to do so? Probably not, although teachers of ethnic studies should consider whether this makes sense in any given project.

Helping students reclaim cultural identities was central to some projects, such as Project EXCEL (Lewis et al., 2006) and *Pinoy Teach* (Halagao, 2004). Ethnic identity and achievement identity were conceptually linked in several projects such as López's (2017) studies of Latinx student achievement and the Mexican American Studies Social Justice Education Project (Cammarota & Romero, 2009). But reclaiming cultural or ethnic identities was not directly mentioned in several other projects.

Much less visible in the descriptions was attention to intersectionality and multiplicity, students as intellectuals, and community engagement. Consideration of students' social class backgrounds and student gender identity occasionally surfaced, such as in Ginwright's (2000) critique of an Afrocentric school reform; we suspect this area merits more attention. Ethnic studies arose in part to make education more responsive to historically marginalized communities; while several project descriptions briefly mentioned community engagement, the only one we know that included direct community engagement was Tucson's Mexican American Studies Social Justice Education Project (Cammarota & Romero, 2009). Finally, while a central part of rehumanizing education for students of color is to treat them as intellectuals, few project descriptions specifically addressed this as a core feature.

In the following chapter, we highlight several current ethnic studies curriculum projects, including two that were the subject of research reviewed in this chapter.

CHAPTER 4

Ethnic Studies Curriculum as Counter-Narrative

The ethnic studies curriculum is rooted in counter-narratives and ancestral wisdom of peoples marginalized on the basis of racism and colonialism. As explained in Chapter 1, counter-narratives offer historical accounts and interpretations that differ from and often counter those of the dominant society. Vasquez and Altschuler (2017) explain that the principle of counter-narrative

> provides opportunities for the voices of people usually not heard (especially members of racially marginalized groups, but also others) to correct erroneous assumptions constructed and perpetuated about them by mainstream narratives. This principle . . . creates a way of challenging the manner in which mainstream scholarship and the curriculum renders the voices of marginalized people mute. (p. 25)

De los Rios, López, and Morrell (2015) characterize ethnic studies curriculum as a "critical pedagogy of race," which is "rigorous and relevant in that it is centered within the everyday and historical experiences of young people and it pushes them to connect intellectual rigor with the pursuit of a fuller humanity" (p. 93). Within a critical pedagogy of race, an ethnic studies curriculum is reconfigured from color-blindness to race consciousness, and students are invited to pose questions relevant to their own lives, then to use academic tools and knowledge to address those questions.

ETHNIC STUDIES AS A CONCEPTUAL APPROACH

An ethnic studies curriculum develops and teaches insights, stories, histories, and other forms of knowledge that derive from historically marginalized peoples. Is it not a curriculum "about" groups. Rather, ethnic studies is a disciplinary or interdisciplinary way of viewing the world from the vantage point of one or more marginalized groups. Although an ethnic studies stance toward curriculum has been taken up mainly in the social sciences, it is applicable to all academic disciplines. A fundamental question ethnic studies poses is this: From whose vantage point was any given body of knowledge constructed and how does it benefit particular groups? Banks (1993) maintains that "the knowledge that people create is heavily influenced by their interpretations of their experiences and their positions within particular social, economic, and political systems and structures of society" (p. 5). Within the Western tradition, knowledge is conceived as objective and universal, so it often is taught without being interrogated. Ethnic studies demands such interrogation.

We challenge educators to think beyond short, superficial surveys about racial/ethnic groups that miss opportunities to critically reframe curriculum through what Banks (1993) terms "transformative intellectual knowledge" (p. 9). Banks defines transformative intellectual knowledge as the "concepts, paradigms, and themes" that emerged through the critical traditions of ethnic studies, women's studies, and disability studies. Such knowledge "challenges some of the key assumptions that mainstream scholars make about the nature of knowledge" (p. 9). Banks (2004) explains, "Knowledge emanating from marginalized epistemological communities often questions existing political, economic and educational practices, and demands fundamental changes and reforms. It often reveals the inconsistency between democratic ideals within a society and its social arrangements and educational practices" (p. 237).

Rather than organizing curriculum around details about groups, then, ethnic studies teachers organize it around key concepts. For example, in *Teaching Strategies for Ethnic Studies*, Banks (2008) proposes a conceptual approach for curriculum that is interdisciplinary and in which key concepts are drawn from the ethnic studies literature. He explains that teachers need to differentiate among facts, concepts, generalizations, and theories in order to develop coherent and thoughtful curriculum. Examples of concepts include origins and immigrations, cultural assimilation, structural assimilation, power, and values. Concepts are supported by facts (such as the number of immigrants that arrived in a particular year) and generalizations (such as what a given immigrant group usually did on arrival). Theories predict human behavior, making use of concepts, facts, and generalizations. Banks explains that concepts are particularly useful because students cannot make good sense of facts, generalizations, or theories without them. As you will see in this chapter, the curriculum exemplars we discuss are organized in this way.

Cuauhtin (2019a) proposes a conceptual framework rooted in core themes within the ethnic studies literature. He outlines four geohistorical macroscales (or deep themes) of ethnic studies that derive from "oppositional stories and counter-narratives that name, speak to, resist, and transform the hegemonic Eurocentric neocolonial condition" (p. 72). The four macroscales, which came about through conversing with ethnic studies teachers, reading the ethnic studies literature, and working with Christine's earlier distillation of the ethnic studies literature (Sleeter, 2000), include:

1. *Indigeneity and roots:* This theme emphasizes "the sovereignty and autonomy of the Indigenous peoples/first nations of the land where the courses are being taught" (Cuauhtin, 2019a, p. 69), as well as the "precolonial roots, worldviews, cosmovisions, perspectives, and discourses of the ancestral and intergenerational legacies of all students" (p. 69). In other words, everyone has ancestral roots somewhere that are worth reclaiming. Further, the ethnic studies class itself is located on the ancestral homeland of Indigenous peoples whose history and connection with the land need to be recognized.

2. *Coloniality, dehumanization, and genocide:* This theme entails unpacking the "totalizing practice of dehumanization, domination, oppression, and theft that involves the subjugation of one people to another; this includes the process of European settlement and/or socioeconomic and political control and traumatization over much of the rest of the world" (p. 70). While colonialism historically dehumanized and traumatized people of color globally (through processes such as genocide, theft of resources and labor, and forced migrations), its ongoing impacts shape the contours of many students' lives, such as institutionalized poverty and mass incarcerations that many communities of color experience.

3. *Hegemony and normalization:* This theme entails examining how "explicit and intersectional power relationships based on colonization [were rendered] implicit, institutionalized, and 'normal'" (p. 71). Colonization and racism, brought into being through violence, are institutionalized in a way that manufactures the consent of oppressed peoples by leading them to believe that the system is fair or at least unchangeable. "By recovering, attending to, and creating counter-narratives from subordinate social positions at various intersections (race, gender, sexuality, class, etc.), ethnic studies engages students in demasking hegemony's (neo)colonial gaze, and creating narratives that question and repudiate oppressive relationships while encouraging them to embrace themselves and their communities as fully human" (p. 72).

4. *Decoloniality, regeneration, and transformational resistance:* This theme engages young people in authoring and working toward conditions in which they can thrive, anchoring their vision and knowledge in ancestral knowledge and counter-narratives, and fully affirming them as human beings. It represents "an awakening and growing of the consciousness of the three other scales" (p. 72).

The teachers in Tucson who worked with Mexican American Studies/
Mexican American Raza Studies laid crucial foundational curricular work
that others have built on.* In this chapter we share exemplars of ethnic studies curricula, some of which clearly are indebted to that work in Tucson.
To select exemplars for this chapter we asked knowledgeable colleagues for
recommendations. We settled on those that exemplify multiple hallmarks
of ethnic studies, as outlined in Chapter 1. You will see that ethnic studies
curricula cannot be standardized, although there are core themes that run
across curricula. While educators can borrow and share, and while there is
a need for teacher resources, ethnic studies curricula must respond to local
contextual issues and invite collaboration with students, their families, and
local knowledge holders.

We organized this chapter into five sections, each addressing a different
student population or curriculum challenge. The first section illustrates ethnic studies in early childhood; the second explores the work of two Black
studies high school teachers; the third offers two quite different examples of
Native American studies, one at the school level and the other at the statewide level; the fourth section presents two different secondary-level curricula designed for racially and ethnically diverse student populations; and the
fifth illustrates ethnic studies designed around YPAR.

ETHNIC STUDIES IN EARLY CHILDHOOD

Currently, most examples of ethnic studies are drawn from the secondary
level. Although there are growing calls for ethnic studies in K–12, many educators find it easier to visualize what this means for older than for younger
children. There are, however, frameworks and resources for ethnic studies at
the early childhood level. For example, the *Anti-Bias Curriculum* (Derman-
Sparks and the A. B. C. Task Force, 1989) has been widely available and
used for decades and currently is woven into the work of Teaching Tolerance
(2014). Some educators come to early childhood education through social
justice (e.g., Agarwal-Rangnath, 2013; Souto-Manning & Rabadi-Raol,
2018; Zakin, 2012) or prejudice reduction (e.g., Aboud et al., 2012).

But there is a robust history of culturally specific curricula and programs designed to counter traditional assimilationist and colonial child care
and education. Black educators, for example, for decades have designed and
taught culturally appropriate curricula for African American young children. Prominent among them was Janice Hale-Benson (1990), who worked
with and evaluated Visions for Children, a program that emphasized early

---

*See Arce (2016) for a conceptual outline of distinct Meso-American Indigenous epistemol-
ogy that informed much of the Mexican American Studies/Mexican American Raza Studies
program.

childhood African American curriculum that included high-level language and thinking skills, cultural pride, and pedagogy rooted in African American family life. One can find many contemporary programs that build on this earlier work (e.g., Newman, 2012). Similarly, there is a long history of culturally appropriate programs for Native American young children. In her review of such programs, Faircloth (2015) points out that while some excellent ones exist, too little attention has been given to developing and researching such curricula. An exemplar she cites is the curriculum toolkit *Growing and Learning with Young Native Children*. Developed through a collaboration between Native and non-Native researchers and child care providers, it contains curriculum-planning materials designed to be used collaboratively with local tribes (Thompson, Hare, Sempier, & Grace, 2008).

The work of Vilma Serrano, a teacher in Oakland, California, illustrates a developmentally appropriate ethnic studies curriculum that serves as a foundation for increasingly complex learning as children mature. Vilma teaches 3rd grade in Melrose Leadership Academy, a Spanish–English dual-immersion school; for several years previously, she taught transitional kindergarten. In an interview, she explained that she began teaching ethnic studies with big questions:

> How can I commit to social justice if I also am not considering the needs of my students? How am I allowing for there to be spaces for joy and child-like wonder in my classroom? With the increased push for rigorous academics for young children, I felt that a huge aspect of being an educator who believes in social justice, was advocating for my TK [transitional kindergarten] students to be able to play and explore, in addition to creating a curriculum that really integrated kids' experiences, families, and other relevant topic matter. (January 3, 2019)

These concerns underlie the transitional kindergarten ethnic studies curriculum she developed and taught over several years.

Vilma nested her early childhood curriculum within a framework developed by an ethnic studies leadership team of which she is a member. The team was made up of Oakland Unified educators (mostly classroom teachers, but some school support staff, like teachers on special assignment who support curriculum development and professional development). The team met for 2 years, initially developing a definition for what the members believed ethnic studies to be, then using that definition to create a framework that focused on the praxis of ethnic studies. Vilma explained that participating on the team was very healing: "It allowed us to be very honest about our experiences with being marginalized, while also centering our work around what we believe would interrupt the ongoing patterns of marginalization that our students are feeling as well."

The team intended the framework to be available to all educators regardless of the discipline or grade they taught. The framework identifies six ethnic studies pedagogical principles:

1. Critique the dominant individuals/institutions/ideologies
2. Divert needed resources to the community, ensure needs of the community are being met
3. Incorporate multidisciplinary/holistic methods, series, models, perspectives, approaches
4. Foster reflexivity and negotiate outsiderness/insiderness
5. Celebrate communal and individual assets
6. Build community and promote healing

Teachers develop their ethnic studies curricula at developmentally appropriate levels for their students, based on these principles. Vilma's transitional kindergarten curriculum represents these principles in action at an early childhood level.

Her year-long curriculum included three Expeditions. (In her school, Expeditions are interdisciplinary project-based units.) She mapped the three Expeditions (or units) against the kindergarten curriculum standards for social studies, science, math, and English language arts.

The first Expedition—*Family* (mid-September through October)—was taught mainly through social studies. It was organized around key questions: Where does my family come from? What makes us special? How do we take care of each other? The Expedition began by inviting students' families into the classroom; their visit provided a basis for several concepts taught subsequently throughout the year. Families were asked to self-identify by various factors, including race and ethnicity, and to describe where they came to Oakland from. The concept of race (*raza*) was introduced in this context. Using teaching strategies such as brainstorming, drawing, and creating graphs, subsequent lessons considered who makes up a family and where families live (such as in a house, a trailer, an apartment, or a room). Finally, students brainstormed and considered the various ways family members help one another out.

The Family Expedition included a mini-unit on immigration. Vilma had three goals for this mini-unit. First was understanding basic concepts:

• The difference between immigration (leaving your house in one place and crossing a border to make a house somewhere else) and travel (crossing a border to go somewhere else to explore or visit, but coming back home)
• Border (a line on the map and in real life that separates places from one another; kids thought of borders as things that keep you inside or outside)

- Map (shows lines that people created to separate places)
- Indigenous (a person who is native to a land and did not immigrate)
- Immigrant (a person who left a native home to make a home in another country)

The second goal was understanding why people immigrate (such as violence, opportunities, fear, wanting to explore other places). The third was considering how we can welcome immigrants and other newcomers in friendly and caring ways. She explained:

The simple definitions were understood by the kids; they were very confused as to why we had borders to begin with and why immigration was such a big deal to adults. For the kids, it made sense to leave somewhere that you didn't feel safe and it made sense to be friendly to new people. (January 3, 2019)

The second Expedition (October through November) was *Community*. Key questions included: Which communities am I part of? How do I take care of my community? Students began by learning what a community is and what makes something (such as a school) a community. Students learned about Oakland's various neighborhoods, particularly their own. They learned to describe their neighborhood by the ethnicity of its families. They also considered why people move and how to welcome newcomers into their community. The Community Expedition included science concepts, such as plants that live and grow in the community, caring for the community's environment (such as picking up after ourselves), and the importance of recycling.

The third Expedition, *Who Am I?*, ran through the spring. It began with an exploration of students' multiple identities. Lessons on gender explored what it means or does not mean to be a boy and a girl, discrepancies between biological sex and gender identity, and the importance of allowing people to choose how to identify. Lessons on skin color involved looking closely at one's skin, learning vocabulary for a range of skin tones, and mixing paints that corresponded to skin colors and tones. Lessons on self-care focused on care of the body (such as eating vegetables and learning basic cooking) and care of one's emotions. Emotional care included strategies for remaining calm, recognizing put-downs (including putting down oneself), and recognizing how one is special. A culminating project was a self-portrait using measurements of students' own bodies.

From this description, you can see how this series of units translated the leadership team's ethnic studies pedagogical principles to the transitional kindergarten level. For example, students began to acquire vocabulary about race, ethnicity, gender, neighborhood, immigration, and so forth—concepts that serve as building blocks for a critique of dominant institutions

and ideologies later on. The focus on neighborhood and community resources provides a basis for subsequent examination of community needs.
Learning strategies of self-care and care of others promotes healing from
traumas of poverty and racism. In other words, ethnic studies not only is
possible at the early childhood level, but provides a foundation for learning
at subsequent grade levels.

BLACK STUDIES IN HIGH SCHOOL

In a review of Black curriculum orientations, Watkins (1993) maintained
that "Black curriculum outlooks are the results of views evolving from
within the Black experience, as well as from views that have been imposed
from without. The dynamics of colonialism, American apartheid, and dis-
criminatory exclusion have been political in nature" (p. 322). In Chapter
2, we examined the narrow and fragmented shaping of African American
knowledge within the traditional, White-dominant school curriculum. King
(2014) points out that African American scholars for decades have argued
for an alternative Black curriculum framework focused on the following
themes:

   (a) counter-narratives about the importance of the continent of Africa and
       African civilizations.
   (b) a Diasporic identity between African Americans and other Black peoples
       throughout the history of the world.
   (c) the political, cultural, and economic role that African Americans played in
       U.S. nation building.
   (d) white allies who held egalitarian beliefs and fought racism.
   (e) the importance of race and racism as institutional barriers to the lived
       experiences of African Americans. (p. 4)

While this framework derives from the work of African American scholars
between 1890 and 1940, such as W.E.B. Du Bois and Carter G. Woodson,
it is just as relevant today as it was decades ago.
   Equally important is the intellectual level of the curriculum African
American students experience. Perry, Steele, and Hilliard (2003) argued
that most discussions of African American student achievement implicitly
"reinforce the national ideology about Black intellectual inferiority" (p. 8).
And yet, "when we choose excellent performance as the goal, academically
and socially, we change the teaching and learning paradigm in fundamental ways" (p. 138). We consulted with the Carter Center for K–12 Black
History Education at the University of Missouri to identify an exemplar of
Black studies curriculum.

At Muriel Williams Battle High School in Columbia, Missouri, Greg Simmons and Molly Pozel teach African American history and literature in a way that responds to these issues. Greg teaches African American History I and II, and a 2-semester African American Studies social studies elective course. Molly teaches African American Literature. Together, they team-teach African American History and Literature and are constructing an Advanced African American History and Literature block course in partnership with Black Studies at the University of Missouri.

At Battle High School, students are about 55% White, 30% Black, 7% Latinx, and smaller proportions of other groups. But since the African American studies courses are electives (along with other social studies and literature electives for seniors), they draw mainly African American students. Both teachers are White; in Chapter 5, they discuss how their racial identities interact with their work. Greg, in fact, enlisted the help of LaGarrett King in the Carter Center to strengthen his teaching of African American history.

A central purpose of Greg's history courses is well-stated on his syllabi:

> To fill a void which has long existed in the regular American History classes concerning the role played by African Americans in the settlement, development and advancement of the United States. In doing this, the instructor would be trying to dispel many of the myths which have grown up about the past history of the African American race; trying to inform all students of the important role played by African Americans in the history of the United States; and trying to develop a sense of mutual respect between African Americans and white Americans for each other's social, cultural, historical, and religious traditions in this nation of ethnic plurality.

African American History I starts with ancient African civilizations, then their destruction through colonization. The course details how the slave trade operated and was institutionalized in various parts of North America (as well as the Caribbean and South America), how African Americans resisted slavery and the varying ways White people made sense of it, and African American participation in the Civil War and its aftermath. African American History II focuses on African Americans confronting various forms of racism after the Civil War and dismantlement of slavery. Like African American History I, the course is organized chronologically, but the main recurring themes center on the active roles African Americans played throughout American life, ranging from political organizing to artistic production to scientific research, in the context of enormous White efforts to maintain White supremacy. The courses emphasize "what history might teach us about the ways to overcome" ongoing contemporary racial tensions, by understanding their roots and past struggles to address those roots.

African American Literature emphasizes literature as an art form. Molly takes seriously Toni Morrison's concern that Black literature too often is taught "as sociology, as tolerance, not as a serious, rigorous art form." Frederick Douglass, for example, usually is taught as diary entries rather than as "a rhetorical piece of work that moved an audience to action" (November 19, 2018). So, underlying her approach to teaching African American literature is serious analysis of the authors' work as an art form that moves people, asking how it does that and what language and rhetorical choices authors made as they wrote in order to create the effect they intended.

Advanced African American History and Literature blends a chronological survey of African American history with diverse forms of cultural expression that connect current conditions with history and explore social issues and diverse identities of people across the African Diaspora. For example, the first unit explores the varying ways Black identity has been defined historically as reflected in a variety of texts and media. The main text for the unit that explores the slave trade and its impact is the novel *Homegoing* by Yaa Gyasi (2016), which traces two family lines, one in what is now Ghana and the other in the United States, during and following slavery. This is intended as a dual-credit course with the University of Missouri, in which Black Studies faculty members participate in leading seminars. The course also gives students considerable guided practice in learning to craft timed-writing essays that mirror an AP exam.

Overall, this set of courses exemplifies intellectually demanding curriculum, designed in depth from African American perspectives. All of the courses capture the academic demands of upper-track and AP courses, but rather than engaging students with White history and literature, they engage students seriously with Black history and literature. The courses involve regular homework, scaffolded analytical writing, vocabulary development, in-class note-taking, and student-led participation. For example, in the history syllabus, Greg explains to students that in his course, you "will be asked to formulate some of your own historical interpretations. You will learn how to do this through inquiry-based discussions, simulations, primary source evaluations, online research, position papers, and pro/con arguments. The instructor provides foundations, and teaches students to use critical thinking skills and text readings to research, interpret, and articulate individual historical positions." African American History I and II are designed as dual-enrollment courses with a community college; Advanced African American History and Literature is in the pipeline to become a dual-enrollment course with the University of Missouri. As a result of this work, in school year 2017–2018, 30 out of their 40 students (all but one of whom were African American) went on to college.

NATIVE AMERICAN STUDIES

The traditional school curriculum teaches settler colonialism. Native peoples, if included at all, usually are added into a settler colonial narrative and perspective. In contrast, a Native American and Indigenous studies curriculum directly challenges settler colonialism, as it works toward tribal sovereignty and recovery of language, culture, and traditional knowledge. As Dudgeon and Fielder (2006) explain, decolonizing knowledge "involves reconceptualising, rewriting and rethinking what our culture means, how it is expressed, and who has right in determining what Indigenous culture is" (p. 404).

Corntassel (2012) proposes a "peoplehood model" of decolonization that focuses on "the interlocking features of language, homeland, ceremonial cycles, and sacred living histories," and says that "a disruption to any one of these practices threatens all aspects of everyday life" (p. 89). A peoplehood model aims toward decolonization through self-determination and resurgence, or "reconnecting with homelands, cultures, and communities" (p. 97). Corntassel further cautions against investing energy in distractions that attempt to reframe "community relationships in state-centric terms" (p. 91). These distractions include (1) rights rather than responsibilities (rights derive from state-centered thinking); (2) reconciliation rather than resurgence (reconciliation derives from Western religion); and (3) resources rather than relationships (the language of resources derives from the market economy). While his discussion of this model did not specifically address curriculum, we find this land-based model useful.

Examples of Native American studies curricula exist in various forms. In what follows, we feature Montana's Indian Education for All curriculum, and Native American literature for 6th grade from the Native American Community Academy in Albuquerque, New Mexico.

Indian Education for All in Montana

In 1999, the state of Montana passed the Indian Education for All Act, which operationalized an earlier "constitutional mandate to integrate Indian Education across the curriculum" (Carjuzaa, Baldwin, & Munson, 2015, p. 202). Two years later, Indigenous educators, scholars, and leaders collaborated to develop seven Essential Understandings (Stanton & Morrison, 2018); they drew on Banks's (1999) model of curriculum integration, discussed in Chapter 2. Stanton and Morrison explain that advocates of Indian Education for All "noted the importance of *transforming* the curriculum across grade levels and content areas for all students, not just Indigenous students" (p. 734, emphasis in the original).

In 2005, the state of Montana committed funds to support curriculum writing and professional development based on the Essential Understandings.

Hundreds of lesson plans can now be accessed on the Indian Education webpage of the state's Office of Public Instruction (opi.mt.gov/Educators/Teaching-Learning/Indian-Education). They are organized by subject area (art, health enhancement, language arts & literature, mathematics, music, science, and social studies) and grade level (pre-K–2, 3–5, 6–8, and 9–12), and several are accompanied by resources teachers can use. Development of the lesson plans, downloadable as PDF files, was supported with state funding and guided and vetted by the Office of Indian Education. They are all directly connected with at least one Essential Understanding, as well as the Montana CCSS. They encourage teachers to develop plans to Banks's (1999) transformational and social action levels of curriculum integration. The state also provides "professional development for school administrators, curriculum directors, IEFA coaches, K–12 teachers, librarians, school boards, law enforcement, and other community groups" (Carjuzaa et al., 2015, p. 203).

Two things stand out for our discussion of ethnic studies curriculum: the importance of a well-thought-out curriculum framework that is consistent with tribal sovereignty, land reclamation, and cultural resurgence; and use of that framework to guide curriculum and professional development across the subject areas and grade levels. Montana's seven Essential Understandings serve as the organizing framework for curriculum. For example, an Essential Understanding that focuses on land is:

> 4. Reservations are lands that have been reserved by the tribes for their own use through treaties, statutes, and executive orders and were not "given" to them. The principle that land should be acquired from the Indians only through their consent with treaties involved three assumptions: I. Both parties to treaties were sovereign powers. II. Indian tribes had some form of transferable title to the land. III. Acquisition of Indian lands was solely a government matter not to be left to individual colonists.

An Essential Understanding that focuses on cultural resurgence is:

> 3. The ideologies of Native traditional beliefs and spirituality persist into modern day life as tribal cultures, traditions, and languages are still practiced by many American Indian people and are incorporated into how tribes govern and manage their affairs. Additionally, each tribe has its own oral histories, which are as valid as written histories. These histories pre-date the "discovery" of North America.

One focusing on sovereignty and relationships is:

7. Under the American legal system, Indian tribes have sovereign powers, separate and independent from the federal and state governments. However, the extent and breadth of tribal sovereignty is not the same for each tribe.

While the lesson plans are all written to at least one Essential Understanding, because they are organized by grade level and subject area, we had some difficulty tracing how each Essential Understanding was developed. For example, in order to figure out how No. 4 was developed, Christine had to hunt by lesson plan title, then download and skim lesson plans. It appears that at present some of the Essential Understandings have received more curricular attention than others.

Nonetheless, there are tremendous resources available to Montana teachers. For example, in a 4th-grade lesson plan on ecosystems, students study Indian knowledge of the local ecosystem, including concepts such as using plants respectfully. Students read stories such as *Between Earth & Sky: Legends of Native American Sacred Places* by Joseph Bruchac and Thomas Locker (1999), which are connected with content about ecosystems. As another example, a high school social studies lesson compares American Indian and European economic systems. The lesson plan itself is sketchy, but it points teachers toward several extensive online and print resources to work with. One of these is an interactive website (*Campfire Stories with George Catlin*) that features a comparison of European individualism and American Indian communalism, showing how each sets up a different kind of relationship with the land.

Research is beginning to find Montana's model having a constructive impact on teachers. Stanton and Morrison (2018) report two case studies. One case study compares the curricular decisionmaking of two high school social studies teachers who teach in similar rural communities: one in Montana and the other in Wyoming, which has no comparable curriculum. They found that Montana's Indian Education for All curriculum enables teachers to "access and integrate Indigenous counter-narratives into their curricula" (p. 738), in contrast to Wyoming teachers. The Montana teacher in their study "acknowledges that without the state's policy and support, she probably would not even know about the stories herself, as she notes she does not personally have Indigenous friends or mentors" (p. 740). The second case study examined Indian education in a preservice teacher education program in Montana. There, the researchers found attention to Indigenous peoples in curriculum sporadic at best. They concluded that tools such as Indian Education for All can support the transformation of curriculum by making resources and counter-narratives available, as long as teachers (and teacher educators) are willing to make use of them. But they caution that "to advance deconstruction of settler-colonial curricula, teachers also need to take ownership of their own learning within and beyond the classroom" (p. 743).

Native American Literature in Middle School

Valerie Siow (Pueblo of Laguna) shared the 6th-grade Native American literature curriculum she designed and taught at the Native American Community Academy in Albuquerque, New Mexico. NACA is a public charter school that serves middle and high school students; about 95% identify as Native American from about 60 different Native nations (McCarty & Lee, 2014). McCarty and Lee explain that "NACA's mission is to provide a holistic or well-rounded education focused on 'strengthening communities by developing strong leaders who are academically prepared, secure in their identity and healthy'" (p. 108). The school's core values of "respect, responsibility, community/service, culture, perseverance, and reflection . . . reflect those held in NACA students' tribal communities" (p. 108). The curriculum features "the state-required courses in math, English reading and writing, science, and social studies," developed through Native perspectives and knowledge "while attending to state standards" (p. 111). Indigenous languages (Navajo, Lakota, and Tewa) also are taught. We were interested in NACA because, as McCarty and Lee explain, it has become recognized as a model of balancing federal and state education requirements with culturally sustaining and revitalizing Indigenous education.

Valerie taught Native literature and humanities at NACA for 9 years and now supports leaders of schools that are members of the NACA Inspired Schools Network. She shared with us why a Native studies curriculum is important to her personally:

> I didn't really so much as know the history of Native people,
> the Indigenous people outside my own community because my
> community, we're still in our homeland, we're still really close to those
> spaces that tie us back . . . to our creation story, our origin story. And
> so I didn't know until I got to college the Trail of Tears, the Allotment
> Act, and all those things that happened to Indigenous people on this
> continent. And to me, that was an injustice. Why did it have to take
> me going away to school, me paying for an education to even get this
> kind of information? And that really, you know . . . that makes me
> mad to this day. . . . I knew that I never wanted another Native child
> to feel that way, to question their ability or to question their worth.
> (February 19, 2019)

Valerie explained that NACA uses *Understanding by Design* (Wiggins & McTighe, 2005) to connect Native knowledge and perspectives with CCSS: "We had thought before, you know, planning units with the essential questions on understanding. And we worked on that until we were finally able to do a year-round curriculum, to be able to have a year-round essential question." She did not see CCSS as an obstacle because "it doesn't dictate what texts you have to use, so as long as you're meeting those benchmarks. So for us, that was helpful because we got to choose the texts." However, finding good Native literature for 6th grade was a challenge:

> I never heard of anyone doing Native lit at the middle school level. . . . So it was a challenge, determining what texts we were gonna see. But it's really nice over time because now there's so many more titles to choose from. It's becoming a genre that more authors are writing and citing about. (February 19, 2019)

NACA's curriculum plan for 6th-grade Native American literature identifies the big idea students gain as: "read, discuss and write about the texts they encounter in Native literature so that in the long run, on their own, they will be able to recognize that reading, writing and thinking skills are valuable resources for leading and serving Native communities." The curriculum focuses on story, which Valerie explained is particularly important to Native people: "In our own Indigenous society that's how we pass our past knowledge, essentially."

In designing the curriculum, she explained: "I divided it into skills and content. So my content focused on why do we have stories, and my skill essential question was, what elements do all stories have in common? So I was able to ask students, even go back and consider the stories that are shared intergenerationally with their parents, grandparents. Those stories all matter, and those can be looked at as text" (February 19, 2019).

The curriculum consists of four units, with the skills for each unit based mainly in CCSS, and the content mainly in Native stories. Unit 1 features two main pieces of literature: *Our Stories Remember* (Joseph Bruchac, 2003) and *How I Became a Ghost* (Tim Tingle, 2013). Students learn about two types of traditional stories (creation and values), as well as the transformative power of story. In Unit 2, students read *The Whale Rider* (Witi Ihimaera, 2005) and the Zuni Salt Lake story. Here, they dig into the use of words and imagery, they learn about sacred spaces/places that have stories sustaining and protecting them, and they consider the role stories play in sustaining Indigenous identities. In Unit 3, students read *Bird Girl and the Man Who Followed the Sun* (Velma Wallis, 1997). In this unit, they examine the idea of perspective, and points of view of characters. As one application of that idea, they analyze how a fictional character would respond to a real-life current event, applying evidence to justify their perspective. Finally, in Unit 4, students read two essays that are easily found online: Sherman Alexie's "The Unauthorized Autobiography of Me" and Virginia Driving Hawk Sneve's "The Medicine Bag." In this final unit, they examine symbolism and synthesize what they have learned about what Native literature is.

Students complete two culminating performance tasks. First is a digital portfolio that showcases samples of work related to Native literature texts explored throughout the year. Second is a reflection on the question: What is my story as a reader and writer?

Valerie explained that it took a long time to design this curriculum: "It took 9 years of teaching at NACA to finally feel that I had developed a cohesive unit that allowed students to think about their own stories, they both [authors' and students' stories] matter, the stories that are in their families." But in the end, the 2015–2016 academic year—her last year teaching at NACA—was her "best year of teaching. And that was when I thought I had really finally developed a cohesive space for Native lit."

ETHNIC STUDIES WITH DIVERSE STUDENTS

What might an ethnic studies curriculum look like when designed to speak to experiences of multiple racial and ethnic groups, particularly when the students are racially and ethnically diverse? Is a survey of ethnic groups a reasonable curriculum design, or does the survey approach miss examining how race operates across groups?

In a review of diversity versus empowerment models of education, Swartz (2009) explained that "diversity . . . has become a code for referring to historically marginalized cultures and groups" in a way that does not challenge dominant narratives (p. 1048). Conversely, an empowerment curriculum begins with questions that are critical to the communities in which teaching takes place. "Knowledge is viewed as relational, created in cultural contexts, and informed by multiple ways of knowing. And instruction that taps into these tenets, ontological orientations, and views of knowledge is typically organized with the assumption that learning is group focused rather than individualistic" (p. 1065). Curriculum is contextualized, co-constructed, and designed around critical questions. Duncan-Andrade and Morrell (2008) propose "critical pan-ethnic studies" that begins "with the relationship between racialization in U.S. society and the dehumanization of students of color attending urban schools" (p. 134). The focus "is on the collective struggle for racial and economic justice that includes members of all ethnic groups while still holding race and ethnicity as central to understanding power and privilege in society" (p. 138).

In this section we feature two exemplar curricula designed and taught for racially and ethnically diverse student populations. Both are high school curricula, and both are located in California. The first exemplar features the work of a longstanding ethnic studies teacher in southern California; the second features a districtwide program in San Francisco.

A Long-Time Ethnic Studies Teacher in Los Angeles

With community pressure, the Los Angeles Unified School District (LAUSD) school board, serving over 600,000 students, passed a motion in 2014 to make ethnic studies a graduation requirement. Two years later, legislation policy for the design of a model statewide ethnic studies curriculum was passed, which targets completion of this model curriculum by 2020. Luis Alejo, who authored this legislation, is featured in Chapter 6. While these efforts are commendable in moving ethnic studies forward in a highly diverse state with the largest number of students enrolled in K–12 public schools, educators such as Ron Espiritu have been teaching ethnic studies courses, typically as electives, for years.

Ron is a seasoned ethnic studies educator who has worked in LAUSD and in other districts over the past 2 decades. He teaches ethnic studies and Latinx/Black studies at Camino Nuevo Miramar High School in the Downtown LA/West Lake, MacArthur Park neighborhood. Grounded in Chicanx/Latinx studies, and an integral member of various grassroots teacher organizations, Ron designed a 10th-grade ethnic studies curriculum that draws from and develops three major strengths: interdisciplinarity, intersectionality, and project-based pedagogy. Reflecting the diverse demographic of urban South Los Angeles, which historically has been working-class African American and Mexican American, Ron's approach to ethnic studies draws from this historic diversity and the intersections across difference, with an emphasis on the common struggles people of color have experienced as a result of a common colonial and racial tapestry.

But he does not teach race and racism in isolation from other forms of oppression. In the spirit of anti-oppressive pedagogy (Kumashiro, 2000), urban educators like Ron use hip-hop pedagogies (see Akom, 2009; Love, 2014) to address the intersection of race, gender, class, and sexuality, among other forms of difference, by centering the urban realities of youth. Such educators aim toward critical consciousness, working through music, art, and other forms of creative expression.

While designed like a survey course, Ron notes the adaptive and responsive nature of curriculum: "These units are not necessarily in order but will be covered in varying levels of depth depending on the students' background knowledge, experiences, and interests." Drawing upon rich and complex histories, such units include "The Maya: A Study of the Popul Vuh and the Fight for Cultural Survival" and "The Dreaded Middle Passage: A Study of Enslavement and Colonialism," which tie nicely to more contemporary and intersecting movements: "Black and Brown Unity Through the Study of Afro-Latinx History," "Third World Feminism, Gender Studies, and Queer Theory," and "The Prison Industrial Complex, the School to Prison Pipeline, and Critical Resistance." A careful review of these themes points to their generative character: His curriculum equips students with tools for analyzing the past, with an orientation toward understanding present institutions and movements historically.

Interdisciplinarity is a strength that reflects the diversity of urban Los Angeles students' realities. A major goal identified in the course syllabus states:

> The ethnic studies class is an interdisciplinary class that focuses on the history of African Americans, Chicana/os, Latina/os, Asian Americans, Native Americans and other ethnic groups. We will study each group historically in relationship to each other and in relationship to the history of the US.

While interdisciplinarity in education often is defined narrowly as cross-curricular approaches, such as when distinct fields of study are brought together in the investigation of a particular theme, social issue, or problem, this ethnic studies course conceptualizes history and students' experiences as an amalgam of intersecting narratives. Rather than build from fields of study, this course centers the lived experiences of past and present communities, and of pan-ethnic groups, by situating those experiences in context and in relation to one another.

In this sense, some ethnic studies educators like R. Tolteka Cuauhtin have argued for a *trans*disciplinary approach, which also integrates the complexity and diversity of students' cultural and community knowledge, along with their experiences of struggle and resistance, into traditional fields of study. For instance, the unit on "Black and Brown Unity Through the Study of Afro-Latinx History" explores the "shared African, Indigenous, Latino, and ancestral past, including resistance to colonialism." This unit, as defined in Ron's 10th-grade ethnic studies course, is contextualized in the lives of Black and Brown urban Los Angeles youth, who share education and other spaces in their everyday lives, yet "are not often taught about the historical similarities and mutual cooperation to fight for liberation that our ancestors have experienced from colonial times, through the Civil Rights Movement, Black Power and Chicano Movements, and third world liberation struggles."

We also characterize this ethnic studies course as intersectional, meaning that it looks at race and racism in relation to other forms of oppression. Yosso (2002) argues for a critical approach to race studies that takes seriously the intersecting nature of gender and sexuality when fighting against racism. Sleeter and Delgado Bernal (2004) outline working principles for critical multicultural education, identifying Critical Race Theory as a framework to "understand and analyze the multiple identities and knowledges of people of color without essentializing their various experiences" (p. 246). In this vein, Ron Espiritu's ethnic studies course addresses gender and sexuality via sets of questions and themes found across core units of study.

For example, the unit on "Third World Feminism, Gender Studies, and Queer Theory" equips students with tools for understanding their multiple identities, as well as an orientation toward unpacking how structural forms of power intersect:

> Understanding that Capitalist exploitation, Patriarchy, racism, homophobia, and heteronormativity are all deeply connected to the negative impact of colonialism on the world and particularly on people in the so called "Third World" helps us to make broader connections to our view of social justice.

This unit builds from films such as *Whale Rider*, *A Thousand Voices*, and *La Mission*, which grapple with ways in which people of color experience gender and sexuality. Further, the curriculum centers women's lives in very strategic ways. The "Women Make History" unit introduces students to women leaders of the past century. This investigation proceeds to students' interviewing women in their lives as a way to build from their cultural worlds and also to understand how women, whose lives often are silenced and untold, have positively impacted their communities. This unit is quite interesting, as it uses the arts and community projects in which students present their research and artwork (via graffiti stencils) to one another and the community, as illustrated in Figure 4.1.

Figure 4.1. Photo of Ron's Ethnic Studies and Latinx/Black Studies Course at Camino Nuevo Miramar High School in Downtown Los Angeles.

Photo by Miguel Zavala

The emphasis on project-based learning that leverages the arts is a noticeable dimension in this ethnic studies course. Grounded in culturally responsive and relevant teaching, project-based learning is quite promising when students become text producers and take ownership over their own learning. Rather than assess student learning through examinations or standardized measures, ethnic studies demands culturally responsive and relevant assessments—along with pedagogies and curriculum. Ron's curriculum design integrates student-led projects at key junctures throughout the year.

The Afro-Latinx Chapter Book is a culminating project in which students become text producers, as they design and create chapter books based on the common struggles of African and Indigenous peoples of Central America and the Caribbean. In this project students are asked to share their books with their families and other students as part of a community cultural encounter. Two other projects that leverage the arts and research are the Popup Book project and Stencils for Social Justice. The former involves creating pop-up books that represent the struggles by people of color, using text, visuals, photos, drawings, and other forms of art. In the Stencils for Social Justice project students create a stencil and collectively design a museum featuring their stencil artwork that synthesizes the biographies of leaders of the Civil Rights Movement and other movements of the 1960s.

San Francisco Unified School District

In 2005, the school board of San Francisco Unified School District (SFUSD) unanimously passed a resolution to explore the creation of ethnic studies and to authorize resources for a group of teachers to spend the 2007–2008 school year laying the foundation for a 9th-grade historically based ethnic studies course. During Summer 2007, with support from a university ethnic studies faculty member, teachers began to design the course, which was first taught during the 2008–2009 school year. By 2018, the course was being offered in every high school in the district, along with regular professional development for teachers and support staff in grades 6–12. For more information about construction of the program itself, see Beckham and Concordia (2019). Here, we focus on the curriculum.

Initially, the teachers planned the 9th-grade ethnic studies curriculum around specific racial and ethnic groups' experiences. But as they quickly discovered the impossibility of covering effectively the many histories, experiences, and lives of San Francisco's highly diverse population, they shifted toward creating a framework that enables large, interrelated concepts that center on race and racism to be taught in relationship to local contexts and teachers' own students. The course, which we see as an excellent example of criticality, now consists of six units, organized around the following key concepts: (1) identity and narrative, (2) systems and power, (3) hegemony and counterhegemony, (4) humanization and dehumanization, (5) causality and agency, and (6) transformation and change. Each unit is elaborated with enduring understandings and essential questions. These units resemble Cuauhtin's (2019a) macroscales because both derive from a deep familiarity and analysis of the ethnic studies literature.

Looking at Unit 3 as an example, the curriculum framework defines hegemony as: "the dominance of one group over another, supported by legitimating norms, ideas and expectations within the existing system(s) in power." Counterhegemony "challenges values, norms, systems and conditions that have been legitimized and promoted as natural and unchanging/unchangeable by the dominant class in society." Concepts that support the analysis of hegemony include stereotypes, mass media, Du Bois's articulation of double consciousness, Freire's conscientization, and Plato's theory of forms. One of the five enduring understandings is: "Oppressive outcomes for marginalized communities resulting from current institutions of power can be analyzed, critiqued and challenged," and one of the four essential questions is: "What are the tools of hegemony used in the United States and how do they empower or disempower groups within society?" An extensive collection of resources for teachers (including sample syllabi, PowerPoints, readings, films, and graphic organizers) is available on Google Drive. The resources are organized primarily around the six units of the course. During professional development, teachers learn philosophical and conceptual foundations of ethnic studies, as well as how to use the resources available to them.

Essentially, the course teaches a deep analysis of the institutional structures of racism and how racism can be systemically challenged. As one of the syllabi explains: This course "will explore the critical connections between ourselves, our communities, the larger world and the systems used to organize society. In addition, we will learn about the history of various social movements and how people throughout this country's history have fought for freedom, inclusion, justice, and democracy. We will explore the many powerful acts of resistance to oppression" (Kayumangi syllabus).

This 9th-grade ethnic studies course also treats students as intellectuals. In Chapter 3, we noted Dee and Penner's (2017) evaluation of the impact of this course on five cohorts of students. The evaluation found a positive impact on students' GPA, attendance, and credits earned toward graduation. It also found that the impact was due to the curriculum itself more than to the teachers, in that the same teachers were not producing the same impact in their other courses.

Ethnic studies represents a way to rethink the entire curriculum. San Francisco's ethnic studies program has created an Equity Studies Infusion Framework to guide infusing ethnic studies content into other history and language arts courses for grades 6–11. The Framework's purpose is stated as: "Our students will analyze and critique existing systems of power (white supremacy, patriarchy, capitalism, hetero-normativity, xenophobia) from the standpoint of historically dispossessed, disenfranchised, exploited and marginalized groups in order to create a more just, equitable and democratic society." Here, following an intersectional approach, deep analysis of systemic racism is connected with analysis of multiple systems of power, in which students explore various narratives about who they/we are, systems of power and privilege, examples of allyship and solidarity, and solution-based praxis. Sixth-grade courses (Ancient Civilizations and English Language Arts), for example, explore these essential questions:

1. How do our individual perspectives shape the way we experience the world?
2. What happens when different perspectives lead to divergent understandings?
3. How can differing perspectives be mediated?

Both of these curricula—one of them at the level of an individual teacher and the other at the level of a large school district—illustrate beautifully an ethnic studies curriculum designed for diverse student groups. Organized around core ideas of concern to communities of color, and working with intersectionality and multiplicity, they make clear the strong overlap between ethnic studies and critical multicultural education (May & Sleeter, 2010).

YOUTH PARTICIPATORY ACTION RESEARCH AND ETHNIC STUDIES

Youth participatory action research, which grows out of community-based education, has flourished into a recognized field (see Akom, Cammarota, & Ginwright, 2008; Cammarota & Fine, 2010). Rooted in the idea that learning takes place across boundaries, YPAR challenges traditional approaches that enclose learning within the four walls of the classroom. While many ethnic studies curricula conceptualize learning spaces as porous, drawing heavily from the lived experiences of students and community cultural knowledge, YPAR is distinct in its impetus toward social action. But rather than frame YPAR as merely "community organizing" or "community-based" learning, YPAR pedagogies address the mediation of learning and the formation of a critical social consciousness in both classroom spaces and spaces where students' research takes them.

In Santa Ana, a major urban immigrant community within a predominantly conservative and White California county, YPAR has taken root in ethnic studies elective courses and in alternative education projects supported by nonprofits or universities. One such project is the Ethnic Studies and Research Seminar (see Zavala, 2019b), a 6-week program that continues with student action research over a 12-month period. YPAR projects have a common structure. The beginning stages of students' action research projects include identifying problems and issues impacting students' communities. This initial stage equips students with a historical understanding of problems, with naming oppression, and with working toward understanding issues in their communities via key readings and learning activities. The second stage includes research design, defining and refining research questions, and introduction to research processes and strategies. The third stage marks a transition from defining problems and research questions to collecting data in the field and in their communities. The fourth stage typically develops into various community projects and actions. For example, students' research may lead to community forums that educate people on particular issues, to students petitioning school boards about school funding inequity, and to using their research to support grassroots campaigns on tenant rights, gentrification, homelessness, and other issues students seek to transform.

Initially, the Ethnic Studies and Research Seminar focused on historical analysis. Through problem-identifying activities, Santa Ana students collectively agreed on the theme *What is poverty? How do we change it?* Drawing from the strengths of ethnic studies, students unpacked key concepts, such as institutional racism and colonialism, in their investigation of poverty. These investigations were mediated by an intentional engagement with such texts as Eduardo Galeano's *Open Veins of Latin America* (1997) and Rudolfo Acuña's *Occupied America* (2007). These texts afforded a historical set of frames that students were able to draw upon as they made sense of poverty, what it has meant historically, and its causes. Moreover, learning about poverty from a critical historical perspective was developed via key writing strategies, where students explored defining, synthesizing, and counter-storytelling.

Writing is a key strand of the Ethnic Studies and Research Seminar. The writing curriculum was designed as a genre-based approach in which writing is construed as a vehicle of social and self-transformation. The development of each writing genre was generative in the sense that each key assignment built from the previous ones, leading up to the development of the culminating research project and symposium. There was ample flexibility in the writing curriculum: The topics covered, such as an extended definition of poverty—the first major writing assignment—intentionally built from history content and served to inform the broader unifying theme. The initial stages of the research were defined as foundational, given that key concepts were developed via close text analysis activities, the use of popular culture texts, and using writing as a bridge between key concepts and making sense of students' lived experiences.

Because students took ownership over their research projects, the second stage involved students articulating subtopics or problems that they experienced in their everyday lives—but that were tied to the broader theme, *What is poverty? How do we change it?* Subthemes that emerged included homelessness, unequal school funding, mental health, gentrification, and so on.

During the third stage, the focus turned toward using the skills of research to investigate problems in their communities. Students were taught research strategies, such as interviewing, ethnographic observation, demographic analysis, and descriptive statistics. Teaching these strategies depends upon the kind of research questions students generate—research strategies therefore are taught in relation to those questions. For instance, the action research team of students exploring the underfunding of schools wanted to know more about the ways they could document unequal funding across their district, Santa Ana, compared with more affluent districts in Orange County. But they also were thinking ahead, with a vision of their research informing their school board and other communities, and sought student experiences as important to understanding statistics. After several strategy sessions with input from other research teams and with the guidance of the teacher, the students centered the testimonies of students in the district, whose voices hopefully would attract the attention of school leaders, who often did not understand the impact of underfunding on students in their district.

The final stage of the action research process included moving into community settings, where students collected data. Time was allotted for students' reflection on the research process and drawing out connections to the broader theme that guided students' projects. One way this reconnection between data and conceptual understanding was accomplished was via a culminating research symposium that included a detailed presentation of their projects (research questions, theoretical frameworks, data collection, findings) and a discussion that asked students to relate their findings and reflections back to the theme, *What is poverty? How do we change it?*

In many ways, YPAR transforms the curriculum by making it student-led and problem-based. Students take charge of their learning; the curriculum grows in relation to students' investigations. But perhaps the most challenging process is to move from the investigation of social issues and problems in their communities to solving them via social action. In this 6-week unit, the teacher followed up with two research design teams for over 12 months. One of the teams investigated school funding inequities and used their research in various community forums, conferences, and presentations to the school board. Students' parents became involved in a local campaign that was short-lived and unsuccessful.

CONCLUSION

The curricula in this chapter provide clear illustrations of counter-narratives that embody ethnic studies. We conclude with two observations to help move ethnic studies curriculum forward.

First, while the examples in this chapter (and most in the literature) focus most extensively on social studies, the entire curriculum can be revamped through ethnic studies or critical multicultural education. Knowing history through perspectives of marginalized peoples is essential because students as well as teachers interpret the world through whatever historical consciousness they develop. But adding an ethnic studies history/social studies course to the curriculum does not address the extent to which the rest of the curriculum still maintains a Eurocentric standpoint. Even math, as we saw in Chapter 3 with the Alaskan project Math in a Cultural Context, can be framed through ethnic studies knowledge, to the demonstrated benefit of students (Kisker et al., 2012; Lipka et al., 2005). We encourage schools, and particularly those with large proportions of students of color, to develop ethnic studies across the curriculum.

Second and related, while several examples in this chapter illustrate elective courses that are not tied to standards, ethnic studies can be aligned with standards. The Native American literature curriculum from NACA provides an excellent example. As another example, the Social Justice Education Project in Tucson consisted of four high school courses in which Chicano intellectual knowledge was mapped against and aligned to the state's standards (Cammarota & Romero, 2009). Rather than starting their curriculum planning with the standards, the teachers started with Chicano history and literature, which they then connected with the standards.

Valdez (2018) explains in some detail how as an elementary teacher she designed and taught ethnic studies inquiry, which she aligned with CCSS. She explains that teachers must critically understand "that content standards and textbooks are written to reinforce colonialism," and that therefore, "decolonial teachers must complicate Common Core Standards and curriculum to tell the stories of the colonized" (p. 4). In order to do so, "it is imperative that teachers know the Common Core standards thoroughly" (p. 12). Rather than simply following the assigned text, she developed alternative standards-aligned curriculum and created student inquiry projects that were based in ethnic studies knowledge.

Valdez cautions, however, that teachers who lack ethnic studies knowledge are not well-equipped to recognize how schooling serves as a colonizing force and how its curriculum serves as a tool of ongoing colonization. We echo her caution. Without acquiring ethnic studies knowledge and the perspectives underlying that knowledge, teachers too easily can end up re-creating the (multicultural) White studies discussed in Chapter 2.

In the next chapter, we report and discuss interviews in which ethnic studies teachers reflect on their praxis, including how they think about teaching ethnic studies, how they understand ethnic studies curricula and learned to design and teach ethnic studies, and various challenges they have faced.

CHAPTER 5

Ethnic Studies Teachers' Reflections on Their Praxis

"As teachers, I believe we have to be in active identity work ourselves. I need to be constantly thinking about my own blind spots, my own perspectives." These are the words of Monique Marshall, who over the years has polished teaching units on anti-racist, critical multicultural experiences for children. Monique's words remind us of the need for centering sense-making, reflexivity, and identity development in relation to teachers' pedagogical selves.

While extensive research points to foundational principles in developing purposeful and critical educational experiences for children and youth, so far there is very little research on what ethnic studies teachers actually do in classrooms and how this is informed by their personal and pedagogical development. Research on the perspectives of practicing social justice (see Adams, Bell, Goodman, & Joshi, 2016; Agarwal, Epstein, Oppenheim, Oyler, & Sonu, 2010; Agarwal-Rangnath, Dover, & Henning, 2016; Ayers, Hunt, & Quinn, 1998; Ayers, Quinn, & Stovall, 2009; Dover, 2013; Picower, 2012) and anti-racist (Au, 2009; Kailin, 2002; López, 2008; Skerrett, 2011; Sleeter & Cornbleth, 2011) educators has grown over the past 2 decades. But with ethnic studies being relatively new at the K–12 level, few studies examine teachers and how they make sense of their pedagogical praxis (see Acosta, 2007; Baptiste, 2010; Cuauhtin, Zavala, Sleeter, & Au, 2019; Daus-Magbual, 2010; de los Ríos, López, & Morrell, 2015; Lynn, 1999; Tintiangco-Cubales, Daus-Magbual, Desai, Sabac, & Torres, 2016; Tintiangco-Cubales et al., 2015).

Based on interviews, in this chapter we examine how nine ethnic studies teachers think about the values that inform their pedagogical praxis, addressing such questions as: What are the teachers' orienting frameworks and working principles with respect to their teaching? What are their broader political and ethical stances that draw them to ethnic studies? What pressing challenges do they see in relation to their work?

ETHNIC STUDIES TEACHERS

This chapter centers the experiences of nine ethnic studies teachers. The grade levels in which they teach range from 5–12. Their racial/ethnic identities include Latinx (2), African American (1), American Indian (1), White (3), and racially mixed (2). They teach in California (4), Washington (2), Missouri (2), and New Mexico (1). They include:

- Tolteka Cuauhtin, Xicanx Nahua Cubanx, Los Angeles, 9th- , 11th/12th-grade ethnic studies
- Valerie Siow, Laguna Pueblo, Albuquerque, 6th-grade Native literature
- Aimee Riechel, Latina, San Francisco, 9th-grade ethnic studies
- Dominique Williams, African American, Sacramento, 9th-grade ethnic studies
- Molly Pozel, White, Columbia, Missouri, high school Black literature
- Greg Simmons, White, Columbia, Missouri, high school Black history
- Tracy Castro-Gill, Mexican American and White, Seattle, 6th-grade ethnic studies
- Monique Marshall, African American and White, Los Angeles, 5th grade
- Jon Greenberg, White, Seattle, high school, anti-racist studies

Interviews, lasting approximately 1 hour each, were audio-recorded and transcribed. Using qualitative analysis software, interview transcripts then were coded for general themes. A second coding and analysis allowed us to further refine general themes into analytical themes—which we present below, drawing from interview excerpts that illustrate those themes.

In spite of their varied geographical and institutional contexts, most of the teachers organize their ethnic studies curriculum content via semester- or year-long themes (e.g., hegemony, racism, assimilation, colonization, oppression, resistance, revitalization) and essential questions, with units culminating in larger projects. The teachers we interviewed do not embrace standards-driven approaches to ethnic studies. Rather, they frame their work as starting with students' lives and identities, and providing learning experiences that allow students to challenge dominant narratives, recontextualize new knowledge, and develop both skills and key dispositions such as critical awareness of themselves and their worlds. Overall, the teachers framed their understanding of teaching and learning processes in nuanced ways, challenging binary, either-or ways of framing justice work and pedagogy (Philip & Zavala, 2016). We organized this chapter into three main sections: identity, foundational values, and challenges.

IDENTITY AS CENTRAL TO TEACHING

In Chapter 1 we identify *reclaiming cultural identities* and *culturally responsive pedagogy* as hallmarks of ethnic studies. What these signature practices point to is the importance of identity and culture in ethnic studies pedagogies. As ethnic studies teacher Tolteka commented, "Colonization has done its best to erase [Indigenous roots] from us. . . .We have to reconnect because if not, well, they're just effectively erased."

In the classroom, identity work often is understood as a process students of ethnic studies undergo as they reclaim their histories. What we have learned from ethnic studies teachers is that being culturally relevant and creating spaces where students reclaim their cultural identities cannot take place, at least not authentically, if teachers are not engaged in and committed to self-reflexive identity work themselves. This is why awareness of how identity shapes the self (both teachers and students) and social relations emerged as a salient theme in the interviews: identity as a resource, identity as shaped through their teaching, and identity as negotiated in relation to their students.

The histories of racialization and oppression that impact the experiences of teachers of color can be transformed into resources for engaging students and creating a sense of belonging. Teachers of color are keen on leveraging these experiences. Dominique, who is African American, speaks to how she uses her personal experience to motivate her Black students:

> As I started teaching and I had conflicts with Black students who would like refuse to do schoolwork, I'd always be tempted to say, "Did you know that during slavery we weren't allowed to read and write? Do you know what kind of an affront this is to sit in class and put your head down while I am standing here trying to help you improve your reading and writing?"

She further comments, "If the two or three Black students I have in each period can get any bit of healing and affirmation from this process . . . then I have done some really important work that needs to happen."

Monique, who is mixed-race, also leverages her experience toward creating spaces of understanding, where students feel like they are not alone and belong: "As a person of color, a teacher of color, I can always be the one—there's a couple of kids of color in my class—I can be the one where I can use myself as an example as an adult. I can say, 'Yes, when I was 8 years old and I was a kid of color,' and it makes it safer for the kids of color."

Ethnic studies classrooms are spaces that influence teachers' sense of self. Given the nature of topics covered in such courses, with race and culture as core constructs, it's not surprising that ethnic studies is also a space for teachers reflecting upon who they are. Aimee, a Latina high school teacher in San Francisco, who was raised by a White family, speaks to this process:

So, [teaching ethnic studies] really forced me to examine my own identity, which again I think is another key component of ethnic studies is our own critical understanding of ourselves. Myself as an educator, I can't ask my students to uncover things that they think about themselves, how they view the world, if I don't do that work on my own, if I don't bring that into the classroom.

Teachers' own racial identities may position them differently in relation to their students when engaging in anti-racist work. In the classroom, even teachers' own racial privilege can be transformed into opportunities for creating learning spaces that work toward dismantling White privilege (Jupp, 2013). Jon Greenberg, a White teacher in Seattle, comments on allyship and anti-racist work: "That has just always been my orientation, centering anti-racism, reading Gary Howard's *We Can't Teach What We Don't Know* and immersing myself into those frameworks and realizing like it was my responsibility to make anti-racism part of my White identity." This anti-racist work can take place not just as a critical interrogation of teachers' Whiteness and privilege, but also as facilitating students' learning and their racial literacies.

Molly, a White teacher of Black literature, adds, "I'm constantly aware of my racial identity, the fact that I have power inside and outside of the classroom." Yet this awareness of her "power" or privilege is taken up in relation to her pedagogical approach:

Now I'm standing at the front of the room teaching you James Baldwin, we get to have that conversation and I'm there to facilitate it. But ultimately, what you see on the page and what you see reflected back in the text is yours and yours alone. And it's yours and yours alone to sort of figure out, too, what you're going to do with that as a citizen, if you want to be a reformer in this world, if you want to reform the community, if you want to change who is standing at the front of your Black studies classroom, then how do you do that?

Moreover, Greg, who also teaches Black history, owns his own White privilege and moves toward creating dialogical spaces that allow students to interrogate his racial experience:

We want to make the class the safest place to talk about race in the school building. And so we try to kind of open dialogue. And I use the technique of exploring one's own self. And so I let kids ask me questions about, "How did you grow up in such a racist place, yet, you teach this stuff? Are you a racist?" So we unpack that. And I tell them the truth about stuff.

Nevertheless, while White teachers leverage their own privilege in ways that help them motivate their students of color, tensions emerge in enacting ethnic studies pedagogy when students and teachers bring distinct racial histories to the classroom. Greg adds:

> Black kids. They felt like they were cheated, like there's this racist guy. So basically what I kind of outline is that all White people have at least some modicum of racism in them, right? . . .There's a feeling-out period of a good month or so, with kids every school year, of whether or not they're gonna trust me or not trust me in what we do.

The teachers' emphasis on the centrality of identity—their own as well as that of their students—is consistent with the scant available research on ethnic studies teachers. Daus-Magbual (2010) studied eight classroom teachers who had participated in Pin@y Educational Partnerships (PEP) in the San Francisco Bay Area; all were Filipina/o Americans. As participants in PEP, all had engaged in a deep process of transformation as they learned Filipino American history through an ethnic studies framework and located themselves within that framework. They emphasized the critical importance of having worked personally through the pain of oppression to reach a position of empowerment. Studying Filipino American history and doing deep identity work prepared them to bring to the classroom a powerful vision of who their students can become that links students' cultural identity with an empowered sense of purpose. Similarly, Baptiste (2010) studied how three history teachers (two Black and one White) interpreted the New Jersey Amistad Law, which mandates incorporation of African American history into the social studies and history curriculum. All three were passionate learners who were strongly motivated to increase their knowledge base about African and African American history. They reflected critically about their own pasts in order to consider why and how to include perspectives of Africans and African Americans within U.S. history. Coming to grips with their comfort levels with African American history enabled them to engage their students with that history and explore where they fit in relationship to it.

Those who teach ethnic studies need to expect that their identity, as well as students' identities, will become central to their teaching. A person's racial/ethnic background does not matter nearly as much as how critically one has learned to reflect on that identity in relationship to race and racism.

FOUNDATIONAL VALUES

"Everyone's got these cool new lessons but they haven't grappled with their own notions of White supremacy, capitalism, ableism, and patriarchy."

These are the words of Dominique, who has started her journey as an ethnic studies teacher in Sacramento. Her words poignantly remind us that reflecting upon one's values, positionalities, and political stances is vital to the development of ethnic studies pedagogies. Tracy, who teaches 6th-grade ethnic studies in Seattle, also touches upon the idea of becoming grounded: "I think that's what teachers should know before they start teaching ethnic studies. Really reflect on where you come from, your positionality, your beliefs about students and their abilities."

Becoming a critically conscious ethnic studies educator is an unfinished process (Freire, 2000) marked by ongoing self-reflection, intentional learning, and commitment to one's values. Thus, not surprisingly, our questions about how ethnic studies teachers frame their pedagogy (the art of teaching) inevitably led to deeper reflections on the personal and political commitments that ground ethnic studies praxis. Below we outline teacher self-identified foundational values (self-care and trust, critical analysis of racism, students as intellectuals) that inform why and how they teach ethnic studies.

Self-Care and Trust

We asked participants what political and ethical framings inform their work. The word *trust* emerged in most of the interviews when teachers discussed the conditions they needed to establish in their classrooms before launching into difficult and emotionally challenging concepts. These conditions center around building relationships of trust. In that context, some emphasized the importance of self-care because of the emotional work involved in teaching ethnic studies and in transforming classroom spaces into humanizing spaces for students of color.

Aimee, who has been integral to the development of the 9th-grade ethnic studies course in the San Francisco Unified School District described in Chapter 4, identifies "love and respect, hope, solidarity and community, self-determination, and critical consciousness" as "values that we want to bring in and help cultivate in our learning community." Likewise, Dominique reflects upon a core practice, "understanding and loving yourself." "We'll read, and write, and do social justice too, but you've gotta be taking care of yourself as a person first."

Care for the self involves having "real honest conversations" about what students are going through, which in turn necessitates creating spaces of trust. DeMeulenaere (2012) identifies powerful shared experiences and risk-taking as key components to a "pedagogy of trust." His study of trust-building reveals how teachers set up community-building exercises, toward the beginning of a high school course, that involve writing and sharing personal family histories, as well as activities around identity that require students to be vulnerable with one another.

While teachers highlighted the academic benefits of safety and trust in classroom spaces, these ethnic studies teachers' framings point to the primacy of love and self-care in their pedagogy. They do not minimize skills development and cognitive work, but rather remind us about the foundational role rehumanizing relations plays in nurturing the development of students. And this emphasis on love and self-care also leads to a powerful sense of hope and agency. As Monique comments, "I understand that there are systems at play that I didn't maybe choose but that I am part of, and I understand that I have advocacy, that I can move out into the world and I can do something about what I see. I'm not paralyzed in fear. I'm not paralyzed in inaction. I see myself as important. I see myself as an agent of change."

Critical Analysis of Racism and Other Power Relations

Our interviews revealed that the ethnic studies teachers value creating spaces that foster a critical analysis of racism and other power relations. Their recognition of this critical understanding and stance toward racism and power relations more generally is closely aligned with the hallmark practice of *criticality* (see Chapter 1). Recognizing the history of schooling that has served to deculturalize students of color, Tolteka identifies a deficit ideology as pervasive in shaping students' lives: "Some of their educational experiences from K–8 have been very deficit-based, very constraining, not liberating." High school youth "come in with their own deficit mindset about their own community, about themselves, and kind of just like really wanting to get into that dominant norm." Because students have internalized racism and other forms of oppression, the strategy that ethnic studies teachers often take is one of naming the structural and historical conditions that have come to shape the lives of people of color.

In their research review, Tintiangco-Cubales and colleagues (2015) noted that strong ethnic studies teachers have a sense of purpose for teaching ethnic studies. That purpose is principally to help students critique the personal and social impact of racism, and learn to challenge oppressive conditions. Teachers develop this sense of purpose through personal experience, coursework, and/or professional development of ethnic studies content knowledge and intellectual frameworks. Anything short of a critical stance that equips students to analyze the ways in which racism intimately shapes our everyday lives would conflict with ethnic studies as a project. For this reason, the teachers we interviewed are keen on centering a critical analysis and stance on racism in their pedagogical praxis.

Rather than view literacy as a technical process of decoding texts, ethnic studies teachers reframe reading and writing as experiences that work toward particular critical understandings of the world and the self (Janks, 2017; Morrell, 2015). Molly's approach to Black literature can be characterized as an experiential and empowering anti-racist method for students.

For instance, her approach to Frederick Douglass's narrative work challenges passive readings that take it up as "a diary entry." Rather, her strategy is to "talk about it as a piece of genre and ethnic resistance." She adds, "If you just take it seriously as literature and as a rhetorical piece of work that moved an audience to action, it becomes a much different narrative, rather than an account only about the cruelties of slavery."

Other teachers identified moving toward seeing racism and power relations in historical and structural terms as opposed to something that exists among individuals at an interpersonal level, such as when people reduce racism to jokes, slander, and talk. Aimee adds, "I think that in my class, critical means to really look at a systematic framework of what and how our society operates. So, looking at systems I think allows for our students to be critical to those around them, and to really teach them skills that allow them to question but also to have some kind of skill to develop hope and change."

A clear instantiation of this critical yet structural perspective on oppression is manifest in Monique's approach to having children understand how oppression of the past is very much alive in the present. In the context of exploring the way food gets to their tables, 2nd-graders are asked to think systemically and are encouraged to think about all of the people who are part of the process. Modern-day slavery is introduced as an illegal, underground, unfair system that has its roots long ago and far away in ancient civilizations.

> It's been really challenging, really interesting, for me, to have conversations with 2nd-graders about, for example, modern-day slavery. Initially, people are like, "What? Modern-day slavery for 2nd-graders?" But I was able to, when I taught 2nd grade, help young students see that there are unfair systems at play around people's work, the way that people are compensated or not compensated for their work.

As a 5th-grade social studies teacher focusing on the precolonial and postcolonial Americas, Monique is able to equip students with the ability to analyze and draw out relations between chattel slavery and modern-day forms of exploitation of Black people. She has her students understand how these people are "pushed into situations where their work is not valued by modern society and there are things we can do about that, awareness that we can grow so we're not just consumers."

Students as Intellectuals

Several teachers touched upon the hallmark practice of treating *students as intellectuals* (see Chapter 1). For example, Greg and Molly, in an effort to counter the common perception that Black students are not college-bound, designed their high school Black studies courses to offer dual credit with a community college, and aim to have another course offer dual credit with a major university.

Tolteka, who teaches ethnic studies in the Los Angeles Unified School District and conceptualized the four macroscales described in Chapter 4, emphasizes two points relative to treating students as intellectuals that are fundamental to ethnic studies pedagogy. First is relating to students "on a human level . . . respecting students in the classroom." Second is "respecting that they are capable of being young intellectuals." An aspect of Tolteka's macroscales is rehumanization and the idea that we are holistic human beings, which is manifest in his identification of respect for students as human beings but also as intellectuals.

Valerie, who teaches 6th-grade Native literature, echoed this perspective. Valerie recalls how connecting to the literature took some time to nurture. Fostering criticality came about not as an exercise in critical reasoning but was facilitated through drawing out connections between literature and students' lives: "Whatever you brought to the table and you connect the facts to the literature that you analyze and you talk about, to me that was forming criticality. You're able to question, you're able to make sense."

The idea of treating students as intellectuals includes more than having high expectations for students. As Tolteka comments above, it is about a deeper recognition of students' humanity. In their study of the critical literacy development of 4th- and 5th-grade Black boys, Campano, Ghiso, and Sánchez (2013) document the multiple ways children challenged simplistic understandings of race. One of the student groups pursued an investigation of the absence of Black communities in the curriculum; another group engaged in literature circles; a third developed a schoolwide project in which the children designed and created classroom libraries. In these educational experiences, Black children were apprenticed into research and learned to read the world with critical eyes, but grounded in their everyday experiences. Campano et al. conclude that in these three spaces the children became "creators and knowledge generators, emerging organic intellectuals, who employ reading to cultivate critical ideas about the world and imagine a better future" (p. 119).

Responsiveness and Relevance to Students and Their Communities

Based on her research into the practices of excellent teachers of African American students, Ladson-Billings (1995) identified three distinguishing criteria: "an ability to develop students academically, a willingness to nurture and support cultural competence, and the development of a sociopolitical or critical consciousness" (p. 483). De los Rios, López, and Morrell (2016), drawing from three case studies of critical ethnic studies teachers, wrote that teachers' "pedagogy and curriculum development that is grounded in community and culture and includes student critical textual production and product distribution contributes to student critical consciousness, community literacy, cultural empowerment, and humanization" (p. 189).

Running through this research as well as our interviews were the ethnic studies hallmarks of *community engagement* and *culturally responsive pedagogy*. The teachers spoke to these ideas, anchoring their understanding of teaching in a critical analysis of the context of students' lives in and outside school. We synthesize here their applications of culturally relevant teaching, drawing out their reflections on what this means for both students and teachers.

In reflecting upon the development of teaching units, the teachers described finding creative alternatives to standard, linear models of history and literature. The dominant model of history teaching, for example, has been a Eurocentric, linear approach to major historical events, places, and people. The dominant approach to literature has been the traditional canon, with "core" readings drawn mostly from European and White U.S. authors. Aimee transformed her modern world history course by infusing it with a "thematic and concept framework of ethnic studies." This shift has opened possibilities for a curriculum that is responsive to the diversity of students in her classroom and allows them to connect with the material.

> For example, one year I taught a huge unit on grassroots organizing and developed a pretty large unit on Black Lives Matter across the world, and I've connected to work I do personally in Haiti. It allowed me to make connections between the revolution in Haiti, the first Black republic in the world, and my Latino students, and making connections between the history of Latin America and Simone de Beauvoir and what happened within Haiti.

Notice Aimee's identification of "grassroots organizing" as the overarching theme—a theme that works from the present, first, but that draws connections to the past. Her approach, guided by essential questions, is a relational one that presents contemporary movements in relation to past struggles, thus enabling students who initially may not see a connection with the Black Lives Matter movement to see it as one that intersects with their own lives in Latin America.

Moreover, ethnic studies teachers recognize the iterative and dialectical nature of teaching and learning when it becomes culturally responsive and relevant. According to Monique, teaching and learning are dynamic when teachers are culturally responsive. "To me, everything is culture. Any space that I'm in has been made by people, has been created by people, and so culturally responsive pedagogy is, to me, helping young people respond to

their environments, understanding fully the perspectives of many." Later on
she adds:

> I really like the word *responsive* because to me it means living . . . I'm
> constantly responding to whatever's in front, not just the young people
> in front of me but what's happening inside of me. . . . What I have
> to offer this year looks different than what I had to offer last year,
> and then the young people that I'm working with, they have different
> things to offer, so I feel like all curriculum, the best kind of learning,
> is responsive. Responsive to the environment, responsive to the issues
> that are coming up, responsive to the people that are in front of me as
> a teacher, as a community that's being built in the classroom.

Her reflection on culture as situated, changing, and central to social
life parallels sociocultural theories of learning (Cole, 1998; John-Steiner &
Mahn, 1996). Because contexts are always shifting and changing, ethnic
studies teachers tend to operate with themes that are flexible enough to capture such change. Rather than prioritize scripted lessons or regard history
and literature as fixed, these ethnic studies teachers conceptualize teaching
artifacts as resources and tools for learning—and their utility is context-
specific, based on the places where ethnic studies pedagogies get enacted and
the students they serve.

The notion of cultural relevance usually is conceived in relation to students. But given the relational interconnectedness of learning, ethnic studies
teachers also re-position themselves in this matrix, as integral to a community of learners. Culturally relevant practices can bridge learning for *both*
teachers *and* students. Valerie, who is Laguna Pueblo and works closely
with Native and urban students from New Mexico, speaks to the integration of stories in her approach to Native literature:

> I wanted [the classroom] to be a safe space where they could explore
> their stories and if they didn't know they could find out. And I thought
> that was important because in our own Indigenous society, that's how
> we pass our past knowledge essentially. How we pass our language
> is through stories. And so that was a huge foundational piece for the
> Native literature.

Drawing upon her own cultural knowledge and practices, Valerie's use of
stories became a way to bridge to both students and herself.

The idea that teachers also connect with learning was illustrated in
Dominique's reflection on her own engagement with historical content. As a
new ethnic studies teacher, her "attention has been on the pedagogical things
more than the other things," but she adds that she dives deep into "those
things that interest me personally. So I spend a lot of time just gathering

stories from Black women, and indigenous women, and Latina women, and definitely women because it just makes sense [to me]."

Ladson-Billings (1992) has argued that without culturally responsive pedagogy that uses "students' culture to help them create meaning and understand the world . . . emphasizing not only academic success, but social and cultural success" (p. 106), we lose out on creating powerful learning experiences for all students. Standards-based and state-testing regimes run counter to foundational principles in transformative education that conceptualize education as experiential, and student/community funds of knowledge as building blocks for learning. Disconnected from community needs, aspirations, and dreams, pedagogies of compliance foster human underdevelopment rather than authentic learning, and they make schools irrelevant to communities.

A foundation of ethnic studies is that learning is situated and responsive to community needs, and that it is relevant to students as individuals and their communities as collective spaces. Jon of Seattle mentions senior projects that his students, after studying racism conceptually, do in relationship to the community: "Students get to learn about an issue of their choice, then take action on it. So a lot of action is embedded in this class, so they're not just leaving class demoralized." Valerie in Albuquerque described a writing project that becomes "something that you're doing with the community in the community. And I think that is really powerful in terms of not just the students' experience but the community's experience."

Hence we see a gravitational pull in ethnic studies toward place-based pedagogies, which can be characterized as education projects that address students' cultural, historical, and geographical biographies (Ball & Lai, 2006; Gruenewald, 2003). For instance, the ethnic studies curriculum growing out of Sacramento is grounded in themes tied to the history of Sacramento and its development (González, Rosendo-Servín, & Williams, 2019); and the Native American Community Academy curriculum (see Chapter 4) draws from Native histories of New Mexico.

Finally, central to being culturally relevant and responsive is to connect to students. Ethnic studies may render relationships with students even more significant than they are in other fields. Developing caring, mentoring relationships between teachers and their students is vital to student learning (Liou, Martinez, & Rotheram-Fuller, 2016). Ethnic studies teachers build upon what scholars (Newcomer, 2018) have termed "funds of caring," which are foundational to engagement and learning. Thus, based on our interviews, we see three important practices that help further define how connecting with students mediates culturally relevant and responsive teaching: Ethnic studies teachers are attuned to students' needs and often prioritize spaces of trust and open communication; they see connecting with students as vital to taking on content and difficult histories; and they are willing to be vulnerable, take risks, and create safe spaces for everyone.

KEY CHALLENGES

Ethnic studies, as well as critical multicultural education and anti-racism, are frameworks for reconstructing school knowledge. By virtue of their political commitments that challenge White supremacy, institutional racism, sexism, and other forms of oppression, critical multicultural and anti-racist teachers have co-constructed pedagogical spaces from a politics of contestation, resistance, and transformation. Currently, most ethnic studies courses either are high school electives or are taught across content areas (as in elementary contexts). As a result, while ethnic studies teachers often encounter resistance rooted in a political stance, our interviewees did not encounter it in relationship to standards and tests. Nevertheless, as ethnic studies is taken up not just as a separate course but also as a stance from which to reconstruct disciplinary knowledge writ large, standards and standardization will become key challenges that likely will bump up against critical forms of ethnic studies (see Chapter 4).

Teaching Difficult Histories in Nuanced Ways

Teaching difficult histories is never easy (Southern Poverty Law Center, 2018). Engaging students in critical thinking, and teaching them to challenge the status quo and to read against the grain of texts and narratives, can be daunting. Teaching against the cultural grain necessitates challenging teacher and student preconceptions about history, the way power operates, why unequal power relations exist, and how they could be changed. Because both teachers and students are products of a selective tradition of thought—the hidden curriculum of schooling—and are deeply shaped by societal norms and values, taking on such ideas as White supremacy, institutional racism, and colonization is never without a challenge.

For example, Greg explains that Black history cannot simply be added into the traditional history curriculum because racialized experiences are distinct:

> Progressivism in the White canon is at a time of growth and all these great things come out of it, but when we look in the Black history canon, it's the nadir, it's the lowest points of race relations during that period. So that's what is always trying to inform my practice is how do I not replicate White curricular decisions just with Black history as the curriculum, how do I de-center that and make it a true Black curriculum decision?

Effective ethnic studies teachers not only have found ways to introduce students to challenging ideas that critically interrogate what they know about history and power, but they also have learned to equip students with analytical tools that engage them with renewed purpose, as students see themselves in these counter-narratives and histories as agents of social change. To illustrate, elementary teacher Monique's unit on modern-day slavery has brought up particular challenges, most noticeably the idea that children are innocent and therefore too young to take on difficult topics (Husband, 2010).

> The typical things that I would come up against are fear; parents or other teachers or administrators feeling like they're too young. A lot of worry about the loss of innocence. When doing any of this kind of work with young people, there's this misty-eyed something, that we want to feel that our children don't know certain things.

Taking on this challenge has meant "finding a way to delve into tough content in ways that are appropriate and are not about scaring kids or creating scenarios where young people and their families are actually pushing away because it's too scary."

Aside from the pedagogical and curricular challenge in teaching difficult histories, a problem remains: How can ethnic studies teachers teach content in nuanced ways? Either-or binaries that neatly carve up the world between oppressors and oppressed, the powerful and the powerless, or that reduce forms of oppression to ahistorical narratives, such as the idea that oppression is the outcome of "human nature," that "Whites are inherently superior to all other races," or that "men play a dominant role in order to preserve the social order," are too simplistic. Understanding racism in deep ways is about learning from the counter-narratives of people of color; but it's also about developing an understanding of both the complexity of racism, that is, how it operates in our everyday lives, and systematicity, that is, how people, ideas, events, and social structures interact and work to perpetuate systems of race and cultural domination.

As an example, Monique reflects on her approach to anti-racist units, arguing for less "sanitized" and more complex readings of the world. "People want to see things as clean, either good or bad, the villain or the hero, Dr. King's the hero, Hitler's the villain. . . . It sanitizes the curriculum." Teaching about racism in either-or, reductive, and simplistic forms is not as challenging, pedagogically, when compared with approaching it from a more nuanced frame: "A lot of the challenge happens when, instead of doing that, we're inviting young people to see everything as more complex than that. Because it's more complex, it's a little messier and I think people don't like mess, so sometimes there's pushback on the mess."

Scaffolding Complex Concepts

Teaching about racism, how it interlocks with other forms of oppression, what its causes are, and how it operates in everyday life, requires a fine balance between abstraction, concretization, and personal connection. Making complex ideas come to life via culturally relevant strategies that draw upon students' lived experiences doesn't necessarily lead to conceptual clarity or deep understanding. There is nothing automatic about how ethnic studies teachers facilitate deep learning—for their students and for themselves. Several of the teachers talked about the challenges in scaffolding complex concepts.

Dominique, for instance, reflects on teaching the Four I's of Oppression (see Cuauhtin, 2019b):

> I tried to transcribe and then do a close reading, but there was way too much information. . . . Then the next day, I broke the lesson into four parts. Ideological, institutional, interpersonal, and internalized. And then I started to build these PowerPoints around each part which had examples on race, sex, gender, hospitals, legal system, and then we dealt out from there.

She goes on to comment on how after several teaching instances, reflecting upon practice, and seeing when students weren't necessarily understanding the ways oppression operates on several levels, her teaching of the concept improved over time.

Similarly, Jon explains that initially, "I just made a lot of mistakes in teaching about issues of race. I didn't have a structure." He sought out opportunities within his school district for engaging in conversations about race (particularly participating in Singleton's Courageous Conversations), and he also sought a teaching position where he would be able to create anti-racist curricula. Like Dominique, making mistakes didn't cause him to give up, but rather led him to look for resources and frameworks that would help.

Molly, who teaches Black literature at the high school level, speaks to the importance of layered scaffolding. The idea of scaffolding, which could be understood as breaking down complex ideas with the assistance of learning artifacts, also can manifest in the way teachers structure curricular units and learning activities. "There's a lot of scaffolding in our classes. It begins with an entry point of a warmup, or a question that's very centered in their lives. Because that is their favorite entry point." Beginning with students' lives, and drawing upon their lived experience, is a core practice of culturally relevant teaching. Yet the challenge isn't to start with students' lives but to stretch those experiences and draw connections to broader experiences and concepts (see Zavala, 2019a): "Then from there, we introduce this broader idea that they might have some idea already about. So here's the definition of mass incarceration. And then they're interested in that." Molly characterizes this art of scaffolding as "juggling necessary skills" of writing, listening, speaking, and thinking—and finding opportunities for students to write their ideas down and to articulate with clarity.

Maintaining Integrity and Criticality

The question of integrity, addressed in Chapter 6, concerns what constitutes *critical* ethnic studies in the face of institutional and historical processes that tend toward co-optation or watering-down of powerful content. Instilling a critical perspective and edge to ethnic studies is a legitimate concern for movement organizers (see Chapter 6) as well as teachers. Tolteka, along with others such as Allyson Tingtiangco-Cubales of San Francisco State University, has been instrumental in the fight for critical historical approaches to ethnic studies in California. Reflecting upon some of the major challenges to ethnic studies, Tolteka offers important insights:

> What's been the master narrative of knowledge, so how can we
> counter-narrate against it? What are the historically marginalized
> and disableized standpoints, perspectives, and world-views? This is
> important. To be critical, to be addressing cultural, historical, social–
> political, economic, and even more levels of analysis.

Tolteka identifies a greater challenge for the movement. Ethnic studies is not just about replacing Eurocentric content with the perspectives of marginalized peoples; it is about challenging its epistemological groundwork. This work involves "confronting systems and problems of power, privilege, and oppression" in fundamental ways. Later in the interview, Tolteka returns to the point of integrity in the face of institutional demands and pushback from school leadership. "People call it strategic compromise, strategic navigation, and navigational capital of community cultural wealth. So basically, sometimes we have to do what we have to do to get by on the system, but at the same time do our best to keep moving that critical ethnic studies lens forward."

Sustainability

Sustainability in the context of ethnic studies as a movement has remained a central challenge. Movement organizers and teachers have learned from past struggles. One lesson they have taken away pertains to the networks of support needed for continued professional development. While adopting ethnic studies as a graduation requirement may come about as communities demand ethnic studies in their schools, who teaches it and how teachers are supported will be vital to its expansion and maintenance.

Greg, who teaches Black history, argues for spaces of support in the context of a vacuum for ethnic studies educators: "Finding comrades in arms is kind of hard to do. There's no mechanism that brings us all together. So like if I go to an NCSS [National Council for the Social Studies] or Molly goes to NCTE [National Council of Teachers of English], there are kind of additives that deal with Black history or Black literature, but there's not a cohesive thing that brings together teachers." Molly echoes Greg's observations, identifying a lack of school support for ethnic studies courses: "Especially that lack of professional development. On the one hand, administration in the district wants us to exist, they walk through plenty of times with the superintendent, they sort of show up to the class. But what they really want is unclear based on their actions in not approving certain professional developments."

It seems that as the movement for ethnic studies grows across the nation, as school districts adopt ethnic studies courses, teacher professional development that is purposeful and sustaining is not yet in place. And this creates added responsibilities for the few taking on this challenge. As Tolteka iterates, "Teaching ethnic studies in a district that hasn't really moved forward within it, you're kinda creating stuff yourself, or collaborating with others you know from the ground up."

Sustainability is also about the critical self-reflection teachers must undergo if they are to stay true to their commitment to ethnic studies. As mentioned earlier in this chapter, ethnic studies is about ongoing identity work and self-reflection upon why and how teachers engage with this field. Paris and Alim (2017) term this the "soul-reviving/soul-sustaining" labor of culturally sustaining pedagogies (p. ix). According to Monique, "White teachers . . . cannot do this work unless they're really investigating their own Whiteness and understanding race-based privilege, understanding their own positionality and then communicating it out loud, communicating around that out loud to their students." Likewise, Dominique argues that teachers of color also need to self-reflect about their own problematic conceptions and how they frame the experiences of racialized others:

> With teachers of color there's some listening that needs to happen from other people of color that isn't so myopic. Because the way that we internalize White supremacy, and patriarchy, and capitalism, plenty of people of color have really, really messed up ideas about themselves, and other people of color, and White people. They've internalized White supremacy too.

Finally, a sustainable ethnic studies project or movement must confront the reality that if ethnic studies remains insular, if it is bound within the walls of the classroom, it loses sight of the hallmark practice of being *culturally responsive to communities*. Aimee speaks to this problem: "Making sure that there is space for community in the classroom. That means being the facilitator of outside and inside the classroom and just making sure the spirit of ethnic studies doesn't stay just contained within the walls of a classroom. That there is space for community as well." Bridging ethnic studies to communities via such strategies as YPAR (see Chapter 4) is vital to ethnic studies projects that address the realities and needs of communities of color. However, according to Monique, inviting communities and families, as co-learners, makes for a more sustainable future for ethnic studies: "I think that parents need to be educated along with their children so that their children can come home and then continue the conversations at home. . . . I think that we need to be partners with parents, and ethnic studies programs in school should be extended to the home."

CONCLUSION

Overall, the teachers we interviewed, provide key insights with respect to three major areas: identity, core values, and challenges. With respect to identity, these teachers recognize its centrality to teaching ethnic studies, including how it shapes classroom learning and also how it shapes themselves. We learn through their voices that identity is a vital resource in their pedagogical and political work. Regarding foundational values, the following emerge as salient in their framings: self-care and trust, critically challenging racism, treating students as intellectuals, and teaching in ways that are responsive and relevant to students' cultures and communities. Finally, their discussion of key challenges points to teaching and learning processes, integrity of the curriculum, and sustainable practices.

Of these insights, the question of sustainability of the movement remains a vital challenge and problem to be solved. Ethnic studies projects are currently under attack. Valerie, who works with Native students, identifies the present political climate as one that challenges difference. Yet for Native communities, "I think our society just really needs to understand the history of this land that we're on. And until that happens we're not gonna heal as a society and a country."

CHAPTER 6

Research and the Movement for Ethnic Studies

In this book, we have conceptualized K–12 ethnic studies as an emerging field characterized by seven hallmarks: curriculum as counter-narrative, criticality, reclamation of cultural identities, intersectionality and multiplicity, community engagement, pedagogy that is culturally responsive and culturally mediated, and students as intellectuals. These hallmarks serve to distinguish between robust versus weak forms of ethnic studies. Although not every example of curriculum in Chapter 4 and not every teacher's narrative about their pedagogy in Chapter 5 explicitly addressed all seven of these, most were addressed.

To note, we remind readers that our focus is on ethnic studies, which we distinguish from superficial or liberal forms of multiculturalism that have been aptly critiqued by teachers, scholar-activists, and others. In a discussion of research practices in ethnic studies, Takagi (2015) notes problems associated with research processes imported into ethnic studies from other disciplines. The main problem is that while ethnic studies is "an interdisciplinary intellectual enterprise inextricably tied to social movements, political identities, and local/national/international community contexts" (p. 102), most research methodologies are not geared toward probing issues of power, difference, and interdisciplinarity. Likewise, there is a danger with "watering down" ethnic studies, either by equating it with multiculturalism or by negating or erasing its historical rootedness in social movements that have preceded multicultural projects or research that is about those projects.

In this chapter, we examine how research has supported and can continue to support ethnic studies. Teachers may be tempted to skip this chapter, assuming that research is for university people. But we see teachers, as well as community activists and students, as necessary partners in research. Indeed, without such partners, how could research be expected to serve a useful purpose to ethnic studies teachers and advocates?

USES OF RESEARCH
IN THE GROWING MOVEMENT FOR ETHNIC STUDIES

Across the nation we have witnessed a growing movement for ethnic studies in K–12 schools, with communities in Philadelphia, San Francisco, Honolulu, Chicago, Los Angeles, Sacramento, San Diego, Portland, Seattle, and many other cities fighting to institutionalize ethnic studies curriculum and courses. Indeed, considerable research on the impact on students of some of these efforts has been generated, as we saw in Chapter 3. The importance of research for supporting and sustaining ethnic studies was driven home to Christine in 2010 when the National Education Association asked her to review research on the impact of ethnic studies on students. As the Mexican American Studies program in Tucson was coming under attack, did the research suggest that ethnic studies is worth fighting for?

As it turned out, the research does indeed support that fight. Although at the time there were no systematic national discussions about how research in ethnic studies for K–12 should be conceptualized and carried out, findings from varied research methodologies converged in her report (Sleeter, 2011). Research emerged as a powerful tool for advocacy.

In the varied community spaces of struggle, research has been and is being used strategically, yet differentially, depending on the specific goals of its advocates. Policymakers need research that provides concise information that accounts for "both sides" of an issue and that enables decisionmaking during deliberation on bills. Scholars and activists use participatory forms of research, where the goal is not necessarily convincing others, but rather educating students and communities on the importance of ethnic studies, and shaping local ethnic studies programming around local needs—this use of research is closely tied to community organizing work. Program developers use research tied directly to their programs to inform sustainable program development.

In this chapter we pick up where we left off in our discussion of research in Chapter 3. There, we emphasized mainly the research findings. Here, we look behind the findings themselves, into the research paradigms that generate findings and the purposes the research serves. We will argue that methodological diversity is crucial for both advocacy and program development, but also that the values embedded in research paradigms need to be considered in relationship to the values underlying ethnic studies. For example, the use of quasi-experimental research consisting of control and experimental groups, with pre- and postassessments that include standardized achievement test results, rightly has been critiqued on methodological and epistemological grounds (see Lareau, 2009; Maxwell, 2004). However, two such large-scale studies of ethnic studies programs (Cabrera et al., 2014; Dee & Penner, 2017) have proven significant in propelling the institutionalization of ethnic studies across the nation. Rather than prioritize particular research methods in an a priori fashion, a contextualist approach is needed that repositions research in relation to the specific communities, institutional processes, and local goals tied to the development of ethnic studies projects.

This chapter explores the potential of research in furthering the goals of ethnic studies. The chapter is guided by the following questions: What role has research played in the movement for ethnic studies? What strategies have ethnic studies advocates effectively employed? Being mindful of the sustainability of ethnic studies in our schools, what research practices are needed moving forward?

ETHNIC STUDIES ADVOCATES

This chapter draws from interviews with scholars whose research has directly informed ethnic studies implementation in school districts, as well as with school leaders and community organizers who use research. We interviewed nine advocates for ethnic studies, including two academic researchers, four activists, two school leaders, and one state policymaker. Given our proximity and the current movement to institutionalize ethnic studies, five of our participants are situated in California; we also included participants from Arizona, Washington, and New Mexico. Our interviewees included:

- Duta Flying Earth, director, Native American Community Academy
- Nolan Cabrera, professor, University of Arizona
- Thomas Dee, professor, Stanford University
- Margarita Berta-Ávila, teacher educator, Ethnic Studies Now–Sacramento, and scholar-activist, Sacramento State University
- Suzie Abajian, organizer, Ethnic Studies Now Coalition, California
- Sean Abajian, organizer, Ethnic Studies Now Coalition, California
- Luis Alejo, former California State Assembly member and vice chair of the Monterey County Board of Supervisors
- Tracy Castro-Gill, ethnic studies program manager, Seattle Public Schools
- Jon Greenberg, teacher and activist, Seattle Public Schools

Interviews lasting approximately 45–60 minutes were audio-recorded and then transcribed. We asked the interviewees about their involvement in ethnic studies movements, how research has been used in their advocacy, the areas of research they envision moving forward, and general reflections upon the role institutions can play in the movement. We used analytical coding techniques to derive themes across the perspectives that were shared. Our synthesis of themes is grounded primarily in participants' perspectives.

THE ROLE OF RESEARCH IN ETHNIC STUDIES ADVOCACY

That's an area of research that's needed. . . . Like showing data of how it's
effective or helpful, that would really help. Because that's what you bring to
school boards who don't know much about educational theory.

—Suzie Abajian, 2018

A major strategy of localized efforts across the nation has been to leverage
existing research studies in order to garner support for institutionalizing
ethnic studies in schools. Movement activists have recognized how policymakers, whether school boards or state-level representatives, rely on specific
kinds of research in their assessment and implementation of new policies.
However, the way research is used is never neutral; the ideologies or stances
of individuals shape how they interpret and use research (Datnow, 2000;
Fusarelli, 2008; Mitchell, 1980). According to Tracy Castro-Gill, ethnic
studies program manager at Seattle Public Schools, there tends to be an
over-reliance on academic research: "The way we talk about data in our
schools has become so disgusting that principals won't listen to anything
unless you have some data to prove it." The presumption in her statement
is not just that school leaders "need" data to inform their decisionmaking,
but that they regard academic research and knowledge production as more
legitimate forms than, say, the practical, contextual knowledge derived from
teachers reflecting upon their teaching practices.

Also, movement activists understand that institutional leaders do not
view testimonials or personal narratives as being as significant as large-scale
statistical analyses and reports. Activists, therefore, have been strategic in
using testimonials of both students and teachers along with more "legitimate" and generalizable studies. For instance, in the campaigns for making
ethnic studies a graduation requirement in California, Suzie Abajian, one
of the original founders of Ethnic Studies Now, comments: "It was critical
to show the benefits of ethnic studies and to really look at a meta study. I
think that was really a helpful policy tool. So to back the claims that this is
research-based, it's not just feel good, whatever." She adds, "We know that
ethnic studies stands on its own . . . but for the people that you're trying to
convince, I think it was very powerful to basically say, look, this actually is
research-based." The study Suzie Abajian is referring to is Sleeter's (2011)
report commissioned by the National Education Association, which is the
first key review of the current state of research on the academic and social
impact of ethnic studies programs and curricula.

We outline below the three major goals for ethnic studies research that
occurs at the policy level, among activists, and within schools. We argue
that research is taken up differently based on the contexts in which advocates operate.

Research as Attention-Organizing Tool

Evidence does (or should) inform policy. Policymakers are not necessarily educators. While very few come from the ranks of teachers and school leaders, how policymakers interpret research and its relation to ethnic studies is shaped by the contexts in which policymaking takes place. In other words, policymakers generally do not approach decisions from the perspective of teachers who are working in practical teaching and learning situations, or from the vantage point of community organizers, who work primarily and directly with communities. State-level policymakers are concerned mostly with reforming existing laws and creating new policies; how they go about this is deeply shaped by what can be termed an "attention-organizing" ethos. In some cases, task forces or other formal structures are constituted to take on an extensive study of an issue. But in the end, policymakers need to organize the attention of representatives as voting members, many of whom do not have ample time to review an issue and the full implications of what policy changes might entail. Policymakers want to know, as best they can, what the impact of any given policy will be. They also have to consider policy change in relation to funding and broader external pressures that may sway their vote one way or another.

Luis Alejo, a former California State Assembly member and (at the time of this writing) vice chair of the Monterey County Board of Supervisors, pushed for statewide legislation to make ethnic studies a graduation requirement for all public high schools in California. He succeeded in getting the state to create a model ethnic studies curriculum; efforts to make ethnic studies a requirement continued after he reached his term limit. He speaks to the key role research plays in passing legislation: "Any legislator who is armed with research to be able to say, I'm not only saying these things, but here's the research that proves that what we're saying is also true, that ethnic studies could have a wide range of positive educational outcomes for a student." In his advocacy, Luis Alejo identified ethnic studies as a "strong argument" with respect to much-needed policy given the demographic diversity of the state: "It's a strong argument, policy wise, and especially in a state like California . . . the most diverse ever student body . . . in K through 12 public schools." Further, he adds, "The only people that could do that are researchers that are doing those studies, looking at students, longitudinal or otherwise. To be able then to put that into a report, backed by an institution, that we could then use that data and that report in the halls of the legislature."

This function of research as an attention-organizing tool aligns well with positivist research. By positivist research, we are referring to the tradition of scholarly research that seeks to address the question: If X happens, what is the likely result? Positivist research assumes that phenomena exist independently of the knower and can be known through careful measurement;

that due to laws of nature, actions produce effects that can be explained and predicted; and that scientific procedures that are objective and value-neutral can uncover these laws of nature as they play out in specific kinds of arenas. Slavin (2005) explained that "nothing less than randomized experiments will do for evaluations of educational interventions and policies. When we want to know the outcome of choosing program X instead of program Y, there is no equivalent substitute for a randomized experiment" (p. 10). While is it not always possible in school settings to randomly assign students to interventions, it is possible to statistically construct control groups that will approximate a randomized trial. Experimental and quasi-experimental design, as well as correlational, longitudinal, and qualitative research that attempts to assess the impact of an intervention, constitute the scientific method, which is widely regarded as a model for knowledge production and neutrality (Mack, 2010). As a policymaker, Luis Alejo is articulating a pervasive culture among policymakers: the valuation of research that is large in scale and impartial.

Much of the research we reviewed in Chapter 3 took a positivist perspective by inquiring into the impact of an intervention, namely, some form of ethnic studies. Research examined the impact of ethnic studies on students of color, including its impact on ethnic identity and sense of self, and on academic achievement. Research also examined its impact on students' racial attitudes, particularly among White students. Some of the studies were designed as quasi-experimental studies using control groups, along with pre- and postassessments, but many did not use control groups, and some did not use a preassessment. Nonetheless, their purpose was to show how ethnic studies impacts students. Most of the higher education studies sought correlation between course-taking and student racial attitudes, through the use of surveys. But even the small qualitative case studies, by and large, sought to determine what impact an ethnic studies course, or unit within a course, had on students. As we will argue later in this chapter, qualitative research has considerable value for ethnic studies, but for purposes other than trying to establish a generalizable impact of a program on students.

To probe into the value of attention-organizing research, we interviewed two key scholars, Nolan Cabrera at the University of Arizona and Thomas Dee at Stanford University. Their studies of the Tucson Unified School District (TUSD) and the San Francisco Unified School District's ethnic studies programs (Chapter 4), respectively, have been used extensively, given that they are the only districtwide studies of the impact of ethnic studies programs. Both scholars concur on the precepts of positivist social science for policy advocacy. Nolan Cabrera asserts that it was important to assume the stance of an "objective neutral social science researcher" when undertaking the study commissioned by the Special Master on the 40-year-old TUSD desegregation court order. "And keep in mind that part of the advocacy meant that my coauthors and I, while doing the research itself, really did take on the role of that objective neutral social science researcher." While such a stance can be seen as problematic, and the terms *objective* and *neutral* can seem "really loaded" to "people who are associated with ethnic studies," the political context in Arizona placed insurmountable pressure on how the research was conducted: Its results were questioned by opponents of Mexican American studies programs, as well as by Arizona state officials, including other researchers brought as witnesses in the court case challenging the constitutionality of House Bill 2281. As Nolan Cabrera adds, "No matter what the results were, we were going to report them. And so regardless of what the larger implications were, we ask a question of the data and we get an answer out of it." Fidelity to research methods and the process was therefore a fundamental goal of their study.

Thomas Dee, lead researcher of the Stanford study of the impact of ethnic studies in the San Francisco Unified Schools, provided a similar framing of his research partnership with the district: "So that's sort of the tradition we came from, that focus. It's an explicitly, and mostly unapologetically positivist, tradition about . . . what's working, and for whom."

Research as Participatory and Educational

Ethnic studies advocates working at the grassroots level have engaged with research in quite distinct ways. Attention-organizing strategies, such as large-scale research studies, have been used widely in local campaigns to petition school boards and legislators. However, grassroots organizers also leverage the cultural knowledge of students and the community in their efforts. In so doing, grassroots organizers employ participatory and localized forms of action research, often guided by students who have petitioned for the adoption of ethnic studies courses and who have enrolled in ethnic studies courses themselves. Much of this work is not published in scholarly journals, since its primary purpose is to organize and involve people, rather than to produce knowledge for an external audience.

One clear example of an action-research strategy is evident in the 2014–2015 campaign to institutionalize ethnic studies courses in the Sacramento City Unified School District. Rooted in coalitional politics, including high school students, teachers, and university students and faculty, the campaign to pass an ethnic studies resolution was sparked by students and the community. Campaign organizers saw educating the community and key stakeholders, such as administrators and the school board, as vital. In a series of community forums, research became integral to their presentations. Organizers studied and presented on the benefits of ethnic studies and culturally responsive teaching, and why it was important for students to see themselves in the curriculum. As the campaign strengthened, faculty at Sacramento State University were intentional in facilitating action research processes that would support the emerging campaign. Margarita

Berta-Ávila, faculty member and scholar-activist, has been organizing at the grassroots level over the years and uses participatory action research (PAR) in her work (Berta-Ávila, 2004). Here she comments on how action research was implemented in an after-school setting at a local high school.

> And so [the teacher], grounded in a social justice positionality, integrated PAR within the program curriculum. One of the student groups took on advocating the implementation of ethnic studies. The students engaged throughout the whole PAR process of identifying, dialoguing about it, doing the reading around ethnic studies and its impact, developing a research protocol, collecting and analyzing the data. And so then this PAR project ended up becoming what the majority of the whole group took on for that particular year that we were mobilizing for the resolution.

The students leading the research subsequently presented their findings, based on qualitative research strategies, including testimonials, at various school board meetings. Margarita Berta-Ávila adds that the university students also served as a support for the campaign, "giving their own testimonies of how . . . they wish they would have had ethnic studies in high school, and the impact that it had on them when they entered the university."

The Sacramento campaign was exemplary in many ways. First, it moved from presenting already-conducted research, to students undertaking the research themselves. Second, while the goal was to push for ethnic studies in Sacramento city schools, the process of education by and for the community was as important as passing a district resolution. Youth participatory action research, when used effectively like this, can be a strategy for ensuring that ethnic studies projects emerge out of the needs and aspirations of historically marginalized communities (Irizarry, 2009). When participatory action research grows from the community, rather than the school district or other institutions, and when it prioritizes the education of its participants, that research can be a powerful strategy in the movement for ethnic studies. As Margarita Berta-Ávila reflects on the benefits of PAR during her interview: "When no students are involved in the process, we are not presenting a holistic perspective. . . . Coming from them it becomes authentic as to why this is happening. . . . In Sacramento we have done our best, after the resolution passed, to hold the district accountable."

The absence of student participation in formulating ethnic studies may, in fact, lead students to reject what others construct for them. Recall Ginwright's (2000, 2004) study of an Afrocentric reform instituted in a low-achieving predominantly Black high school, mentioned in Chapter 3. Ginwright argued that middle-class African American adults constructed a program that ended up clashing with the priorities and identities of the low-income Black urban youth it was designed to serve. We suggest that, had a participatory approach that involved students been used, the resulting curriculum might have engaged the students.

In her discussion of research practices in ethnic studies, Takagi (2015) argues that participatory action research fits ethnic studies particularly well

> because of its adherence to democratic participation by people who are likely to be affected by the research. Research questions are defined by practical, real-world problems rather than drawn principally from academic literatures, though this does not mean questions are a-theoretical or irrelevant to academic literature. Research questions are co-constructed with others and reflect a democratic process of inquiry. (p. 104)

This democratic participatory process is clearly reflected in the example above from Sacramento.

Research as Tool for Program Development

In a discussion of research that would be beneficial, teacher-activist Jon Greenberg commented, "There's no roadmap to how you implement ethnic studies." Districts that have adopted ethnic studies course requirements, and added ethnic studies curricular frameworks and units, are faced with two major processes vital to their continued development and that localized research can support: teacher mentorship and program development.

The first process is the much-needed mentorship of teachers in the design and implementation of ethnic studies courses. Currently, the attempt to open a space for teachers to develop their own courses, and infuse them with ethnic studies content, is a great step forward, allowing for organic processes to emerge that enable teachers to take ownership over the curriculum. Nevertheless, research on how race is mediated by teacher ideology and teaching practices highlights the caveats with this approach (Hayes & Juarez, 2012; Picower, 2009; Sleeter, 2001). For example, in her study of four White veteran teachers who were popular among their Latinx students, Marx (2008) found them to draw on their personal experiences as human beings to form relationships with their students, but they were not able to relate to the racialized dimensions of students' lives (such as their experiences with racial segregation), and three of them held strong deficit views of students and their families, which they attempted to counterbalance through color-blindness. Action research in the form of intentional and systematic teacher reflection that addresses teachers' racial ideologies needs to accompany any professional development experiences that districts might provide.

Another major hurdle is the limited knowledge and experience many teachers have with respect to ethnic studies. Even teachers who have developed content knowledge through courses at the college/university level are not necessarily prepared to work with that knowledge with K–12 students.

Knowledge of, for example, African American history through critical race and other contemporary frameworks doesn't necessarily equip teachers with the pedagogical and cultural knowledge needed to teach effectively. Related is the issue of ideological clarity and the broader goals of ethnic studies. How teachers define and conceptualize ethnic studies varies; teacher-activists involved in the movement have alerted us to concerns about the integrity of the field and to a potential loss of criticality (see Chapter 5). Further, in designing rich curricular units, teachers inadvertently may disregard pedagogical dimensions of learning.

While creative curriculum drives ethnic studies courses and their development, how teachers teach, what they do to mediate learning, may be left unaddressed unless research that addresses curricular and pedagogical practices is integral to supporting ethnic studies teachers. For instance, districts that have rolled out ethnic studies courses can use action research in which teachers come together to reflect upon their own teaching practices. Examples of action research include the intentional efforts by and for teachers in grassroots spaces, which have come to be known as teacher inquiry groups (Bower-Phipps, Cruz, Albaladejo, Johnson, & Homa, 2016; Navarro, 2018). While these spaces for action research and teacher reflection grow out of social justice organizations, this kind of action research can take place within school districts and on a larger, districtwide scale, thus informing entire ethnic studies programs beyond their initial rollout.

The second process pertains to the much-needed research on the design and implementation of ethnic studies courses in schools. Research, when done properly, can be integral to the development of high-quality learning contexts in high-need schools. Research can be a reflexive tool for teachers, allowing them to improve their ongoing practice. It also can be used to document best practices and how they emerge, thereby becoming a resource for improving ethnic studies projects more long term.

The Native American Community Academy is an exemplar of teacher-led and community-based forms of research oriented toward sustaining ethnic studies practices. Grounded in culturally relevant education in the context of subject areas such as Native literature, Lakota and Diné languages, and Native American studies, NACA was founded in 2004 out of a convening of Native communities in Albuquerque, New Mexico. Duta Flying Earth, current director of NACA, provides insights on the process through which the school community has used research: "One way that research shows up for us is almost representing findings or data from another community, and then asking ourselves the question—ourselves meaning the teachers, administrators, students—what does this look like for our school?" This generative approach proceeds by having teachers, curriculum specialists, and administrators ask further questions about "transferability," whether effective practices in other schools can be reinvented in the context of NACA learning spaces.

The preparation of teachers and design of curriculum is a process mediated by ongoing reflection and research. What are the qualities or background experiences of successful ethnic studies teachers? As Tracy Castro-Gill put it, "There's a lot of talk about who can and should teach ethnic studies, whether White educators should be teaching ethnic studies. I think a study about that would be helpful, because I run into a lot of . . . a lot more than I would like to have run into . . . educators of color who just don't get it." She went on to stress that it would be very helpful to know how educators, both White and of color, learn to address race in the classroom.

As another example, curriculum development is not finalized once teaching units are crafted. Cycles of teaching are followed by intentional reflection that is in dialogue with the needs of students and their communities. According to Duta, "There are other layers [to research] in terms of curriculum development. I think the way that individual teachers seek out and conduct their own research, or how [research on the] disparities of Indigenous communities impact[s] our school scope and framework," are ways "that we have become responsive to overwhelming trends and data that's presented about our people." Through this process of teacher-led research, in relation to the families NACA serves, teachers have engaged in action research that has served to inform their pedagogical practices as well as the revision of curricular units. One area they have been intentional about studying is the mastery of particular skills and how assessments can be authentic to those practices. At the heart of this action-research approach are culturally relevant processes and constantly asking, "How does that look from a culturally relevant standpoint?"

The published literature contains a few descriptions of how courses and programs were developed; we and those we interviewed would argue that more such work is needed. For example, Valdez (2018) shows readers how she turned a standards-based, scripted curriculum at the elementary level into an ethnic studies curriculum. De los Rios and Ochoa (2012) describe the process they used to create a Chicanx-Latinx studies class in a high school, then collaborated with each other and with their students to bring this class into the community. Dissemination of more research into the practicalities of developing and implementing ethnic studies would go a long way toward addressing the need Jon Greenberg expressed.

CHALLENGES

In the advocacy work for ethnic studies, a clear set of challenges is manifest. In terms of scope, participants report the need for more research, especially in the lower grades, as well as research that looks at the experiences of White students. This comes as no surprise given that ethnic studies has flourished at the high school level and in urban schools serving mostly students of color (see Chapter 3). There are exceptions, such as in Portland, Oregon, where ethnic studies has been adopted in schools where the student population is predominantly White.

Major challenges for ethnic studies research that emerged from our interviews include:

- Research should account for mediating processes, not just general impact.
- Research should be more widely accessible.
- Research should be context-specific, as schools and communities and implementation vary.

Methodology and Mediating Processes

A methodological challenge pertains to investigating the role of mediating processes tied to learning in ethnic studies classes. In other words, what makes particular ethnic studies classes work or not work? What happens within them? In the Cabrera et al. (2014) and Dee and Penner (2017) studies, district-level data were used to compare the academic performance of students enrolled in ethnic studies courses with their counterparts who were not enrolled in ethnic studies. In both studies, significant academic achievement gains were found, leading scholars to conclude, "These surprisingly large effects . . . suggest that culturally relevant teaching, when implemented in a supportive, high fidelity context, can provide effective support to at-risk students" (Dee & Penner, 2017, p. 127). In our interview, Thomas Dee adds that while longitudinal studies are important, there is a need for understanding mediating processes, such as belonging, self-concept formation, and socioemotional well-being, in ethnic studies classrooms. So, interweaving theoretical insights from fields like social psychology can "give us new ways of seeing and understanding the power of these pedagogical innovations."

The need for mixed-methods or methodological diversity has been brought forth by scholars pushing the limits of quasi-experimental longitudinal studies, which don't necessarily explain the effects of context-specific variables (see Chatterji, 2004; Johnson & Onwuegbuzie, 2004; Raudenbush, 2005). While experimental and quasi-experimental studies are useful for attributing causal impact of specific "treatments" when assessing educational programs, they do not tell us much about the role and impact of mediating processes that actually bring about the impact. With respect to the positive academic outcomes that result from taking ethnic studies classes in the San Francisco Unified School District, what specific teaching strategies and learning situations are most impactful, and how are those learning experiences facilitated? Questions of *how* are often not addressed in quantitative, longitudinal studies. We know that simply enrolling in ethnic studies courses doesn't automatically translate to positive academic outcomes. What we want to understand is, *how* do teachers and students co-create powerful learning experiences, through what scaffolds, curricular orientations, and literacies? And when does student take-up of these learning experiences lead to shifts in their development and to positive social and academic identities that enable them to succeed in their education? These are questions well-suited to qualitative research methodologies, such as participant observation and interview.

Two research programs mentioned in Chapter 3 illustrate the benefits of using diverse methodologies. First, we noted two quasi-experimental studies of the impact of Math in a Cultural Context on elementary students' math achievement in Alaska (Kisker et al., 2012; Lipka et al., 2005). Many additional qualitative case studies examine specific aspects of how the program works, such as how it facilitates the work of Native teachers and how it activates students' practical intelligence. These studies can be accessed on the project's website (www.uaf.edu/mcc/research/articles/). A second example is Carol Lee's work with the Cultural Modeling project, which involves shaping the teaching of literary analysis in high school English classrooms around African American cultural life. Lee (1995) reports a small-scale, quasi-experimental study of the project's impact on students. Her other qualitative case studies show clearly how and why Cultural Modeling works (see Lee, 2001, 2006, 2007).

Inaccessible Research

As advocacy for ethnic studies grows, researchers are challenged with making their studies accessible to broader audiences. Luis Alejo comments on this issue: "When you're able to make research useful not only for policymakers and their staff but even for the community to be able to easily understand it and be able to use that, then research becomes a part of social change." Luis Alejo echoes a longstanding concern about the limits of academic scholarship: Studies published in peer-reviewed journals often do not reach audiences beyond the academy. Published articles are written for specific audiences and loaded with specialized language that renders them inaccessible to broad audiences. This general observation also applies to the current field of published scholarship on ethnic studies.

In attempting to resolve this impasse, researchers can develop community-based strategies that prioritize dissemination outlets that school administrators, teachers, and families can access and use. For instance, Mora and Diaz (2014) outline a community-oriented research agenda that places at center the question, "How can [researchers] transfer knowledge developed within academic institutions into specific, community-oriented research that beneficially influences government policy and programs?" (p. 11).

Undoubtedly, local efforts to institutionalize ethnic studies have embraced some of these strategies as task forces are created by school boards that often include researchers working alongside teachers. In these task forces, academics can serve as a strategic bridge between the university and the community, and can leverage their expertise in co-designing qualitative and quantitative studies that directly respond to local needs.

By virtue of the longstanding historical divide between universities and communities, and the legacy of extractive or "drive-by" research that over-whelmingly benefits researchers and universities, a related issue pertains to a lack of authentic partnerships that can seed meaningful and useful re-search. Margarita Berta-Ávila reports, "Many researchers haven't taught, haven't been in high schools, haven't been in those areas, so then there's some dismissiveness." If scholars have been disconnected from schools and have not taken the time to build trust with teachers, they inevitably may find themselves perpetuating a divisive cycle whereby teachers disregard academic work and researchers in turn frame teacher-based knowledge as inconsequential (Zeichner, 1995). Sean Abajian, who helped form Ethnic Studies Now in California, echoes a similar concern with respect to outside experts leading ethnic studies projects: "The key to our success is building these coalitions and having grassroots be a part of it instead of just some rich, highly paid consultant flying in to write a report." Sean Abajian's critique also provides a resolution to the impasse: that grassroots spaces, including teachers, lead the work of designing ethnic studies curriculum, enacting the pedagogy, and guiding the research.

Universalizing Versus Contextualizing

How do we translate research from one community and learning context to another? How can educators make sense of studies based on schools and districts that are not their own? Several interviewees spoke about the need for research that is contextually rich and grounded in local schools. Jon Greenberg, teacher-activist in Seattle Public Schools, comments, "I always take it with a grain of salt, the research says that everything we should be doing should be racial equity focused, and that we need to change everything, right? But change is so incremental." His perspective is important because it asks researchers to think about the embedded and layered nature of the institutionalization of programs, and how implemen-tation and development take time. He adds, "So I have this distrust of data in that I don't think it always causes what needs to happen." His state-ment on causality is a critique of the notion of translation: What works in one place, the impact that ethnic studies programs have, may not show up in the same ways elsewhere.

Duta Flying Earth addresses the tension between a universalist versus contextualist stance in translating from one learning context to another. Rather than view this tension as an impasse, NACA teachers have assumed what could be characterized as a place-based approach to learning across spaces. In his reflections upon experiential education undertaken by private schools and how this could inform what they do in Albuquerque serving predominantly Native students, he asks, "What does that look like when nuanced to Indigenous communities, it's really something that becomes multi-layered and interesting, right?" Taking a contextualist approach even further—what ethnic studies means, how it is implemented, and its local impact—we cannot simply generalize to all Native communities. Duta Flying Earth further asks, "So for a student who may be from Albuquerque, what do the Sandia Mountains mean to that student? And how does that place show up and become experienced in daily lessons at school?"

Because ethnic studies is about education that is culturally responsive and relevant to the students it serves, this foundational principle challenges any orientation toward universality in research. It questions even the idea that academic gains as measured by standardized test scores (which were used in the longitudinal, districtwide studies of San Francisco Unified and Tucson Unified, as well as in additional studies reviewed in Chapter 3) are the best measure for weighing the social, psychological, and intellectual benefits of particular communities; or rather, ethnic studies suggests that test score gains should be foregrounded by how particular communities define what "education" and "success" mean to them.

We take these insights as a call for caution against universality, in support of moving toward seeding research projects that center localized enactments of ethnic studies. While we may learn key lessons (and extrapolate working principles for future action) from successful ethnic studies in places like San Francisco and Tucson, we cannot universalize from one place to another. There are too many moving parts: Some districts have a wide range of teachers prepared to teach ethnic studies; student demographics change across contexts; required courses requirements look different; and the curriculum is not uniform (nor do we want it to be). Nevertheless, this call for a contextualist approach should not be interpreted as a negation of particular kinds of research and methodologies. It is also not a radical contextualization that argues for incommensurability or nontranslatability. Learning environments, as learning scientists have reminded us, do not hold still for researchers: Learning environments are iterative, dynamic, and complex (Bang, Medin, Washinawatok, & Chapman, 2010; Engeström, 2011). But good research that is context-specific also should account for nuance and be able to extrapolate to working principles of critical and strong ethnic studies learning.

SUSTAINABLE RESEARCH AND ADVOCACY

We started with the ethnic studies resolution, but it doesn't end there. And so, we need to really think about sustainability, capacity, and longevity at all fronts—be it the teachers, the students, the faculty, community members. That's important to always be thinking about simultaneously.

—Margarita Berta-Ávila, 2018

How can research undertaken by institutions and funding agencies support the efforts of local communities in organic ways? How can research support the sustainability of ethnic studies projects on the ground? In this section we center questions of sustainable research and advocacy. By focusing on sustainability we reflect upon processes that push researchers, universities, school districts, and policymakers to think hard about the ways research is supporting ethnic studies for the long haul. A partial answer to these questions leads us to rethink the roles of researchers, institutions, and research, and how these need to expand in ways that are strategic and relevant to local efforts, because for some ethnic studies advocates, simply engaging in doing research is not enough: The question of the relation between researchers and community struggles may be left unresolved or is overlooked. As Margarita Berta-Ávila put it, "How do you make sure this [research] can help with what's going on in the community? How do we make that work accessible? How do we make that work applicable to the needs of the community?"

One clear answer that stands out is the call for collaborative partnerships between universities and school communities. Jon Greenberg, for example, sees teachers as being involved, but stresses that "it's exhausting just to do the teaching job, let alone to do all the research during it. . . . But when you talk about what could be done more, it would be more of the universities partnering to help do that research." He points out that university faculty members, although they have expertise in research, very often are disconnected from schools and so cannot do useful research for ethnic studies without partnering. Suzie Abajian said, "There's always informal partnerships where people are invited, like academics to give a workshop or something. But I feel like there needs to be . . . a more established structure." Informal partnerships abound in many spaces. Academic researchers may participate in task forces or may agree to come on board as consultants. These all have the potential for creating learning opportunities and for meaningful program development.

But Suzie Abajian is pushing scholars, school districts, and community groups to envision "a more established structure." One such structure is the researcher–practitioner partnership model (Coburn & Penuel, 2016). Thomas Dee characterizes researcher–practitioner partnerships as a "more hopeful kind of conceptualization." Partnering with two large urban districts, Thomas adds, "I think of these as ways to support practitioners in evidence-based practice and policymaking. At the same time, it allows academics to use our position to shine a light on interesting innovation, to catalyze national conversations about it." Another structure may be more grassroots in nature, such as Ethnic Studies Now, which is a coalition of activists, teachers, scholars, and district leaders. Ethnic Studies Now has been instrumental in supporting community organizing across the state of California around ethnic studies graduation requirements. District task forces are another example of partnerships.

In these cases, caution must be extended, as power and decisionmaking tend to be concentrated in institutions, especially when funding originates with them. Also, even if support structures are formalized, collective understandings of ethnic studies may be undefined, at best, or, at worst, key representatives and organizers come to these spaces without a historical understanding of the broader radical, liberatory goals of ethnic studies.

But it's not just support structures that are lacking: Scholars need to develop and expand themselves and to learn from communities and community organizers. Those engaged in research need to reflect deeply upon their own political stances, visions for a better world, and the strategies that they seek to implement. Constant reflection upon practice is necessary in order for sustainable research relations to grow. One area where researchers can develop pertains to learning how to balance perspectives and suspend binary thinking and acting. As Suzie Abajian reminds us:

> In my humble opinion, I feel that scholars are very idealistic and they're very ideologically purist folks. Usually, I'm generalizing of course, I'm talking total generalization and reduction of what scholars are. But I feel that's the way that they tend to be. But when you're working with policy, you have to know how to build coalitions with people who might not be 100% with you on all the issues.

Suzie Abajian's own experience as a scholar, activist, and district leader sheds light on the need for a particular visionary pragmatism "that places contemporary practices in the service of broader principles" (Collins, 2002, p. 25) and that enables scholars to work strategically, while recognizing that political work is contradictory. Taking on a purist stance, whether theoretical or political, may lead to a crisis in action, manifested in totalizing narratives about institutions as co-opted and hopeless, thus leading to disengaged action. In reflecting upon the challenge with maintaining criticality within ethnic studies in the context of standardization, testing, and other schooling regimes, Nolan Cabrera echoes Suzie Abajian's charge: "If we're being too overly critical and not willing to become part of the institution, we understand that we're going to be harming the students in the process because not as many are going to be able to take advantage of these classes."

Taking seriously a visionary pragmatism (Collins, 2002) and an orientation toward community self-determination, Duta Flying Earth offers words of wisdom about re-envisioning the broader goals of ethnic studies projects. For too long, historically marginalized communities have been subject to colonizing schooling practices. "How long have we molded and put our hands as a community on this structure of schooling? I think it's been relatively recent that we've taken the agency and autonomy back and begun to articulate what this means on our terms." The re-envisioning that Duta Flying Earth speaks to demands that we think historically and in nonreactionary ways. "We're not serving to right a wrong or fill a deficit. That's not the work that gives me medicine or sustenance." He goes on to describe his work as "lifting the genius of our ancestors and our people and our communities that live today and more specifically lifting up the genius of our students in a way that emphasizes excellence and holistic wellness."

The standpoint Duta Flying Earth voices moves from one that is fighting against systems of domination to one that is about community-building and the complete rehumanization of students and communities. This shift is significant as an expression of community self-determination because it represents a political maturity that can teach us about the long work ahead. Boggs (2012) explains, "The social activists among us struggle to create actions that go beyond protest and negativity and build community because community is the most important thing that has been destroyed by the dominant culture" (p. 43). What might research look like that centers community-building as a core goal? If ethnic studies is not an endpoint, how are we working in our advocacy, research, and education to reclaim narratives, histories, and spaces that lead to our liberation?

LOOKING TOWARD THE FUTURE

As we noted in Chapter 1, ethnic studies came about initially, and has been advocated for subsequently, mainly by grassroots communities, particularly communities of color, who see the traditional schooling process and its curriculum as part of an ongoing regime of colonization and White supremacy. Research can serve as a useful tool for program advocacy, program development, and community involvement. But along with Takagi (2015), we ask, What kind of research paradigm is consistent with the anti-racist and decolonizing standpoint of ethnic studies?

As we reflect on the possibilities of participatory and democratizing forms of research, we envision three major trajectories: grassroots-level research, participatory research within institutions (particularly schools), and research led by scholar-activists for policy advocacy.

First, research at the grassroots level explores the potential of ethnic studies to empower youth, educators, and scholar-activists. By grassroots we mean research that originates from and is guided by communities. It is the challenging work that is unmediated by institutional structures. While community organizers and organizations may work with academic institutions, the power dynamic is flipped on its head, with the grassroots owning the means of organizing and knowledge production, thus steering ethnic studies in ways that directly respond to community needs, aspirations, and visions of a better world. In *Decolonizing Methodologies*, Smith (2012) explains:

> In all community approaches *process*—that is, methodology and method—is highly important. In many projects the process is far more important than the outcome. Processes are expected to be respectful, to enable people, to heal and to educate. They are expected to lead one small step further towards self-determination. (p. 130, emphasis in original)

In these community-driven projects research emerges as a community resource and is transformed into shared cultural knowledge.

The kinds of ethnic studies projects that have sprouted vis-à-vis these community spaces include autonomous Freedom Schools in the U.S. South and the *escuelitas* in the U.S. Southwest. Research in these spaces may manifest in grounded ways that often do not prioritize traditional research methods. For instance, qualitative research strategies may include conversations and unstructured dialogue; or who counts as a researcher is an inclusive category that may position everyone, including elders and children, equally or differently as experts.

Second, research takes place within institutional sites, such as schools, in a way that is participatory in the sense that students and teachers undertake it. This kind of research is supported by institutions, yet intentionally seeks to balance power, yielding decisionmaking and voice to the grassroots or to community groups. One potential space for expansion in this area includes youth participatory action research. Imagine the role research could play when undertaken by students of ethnic studies, and how a YPAR model can bring in community experiences and stories to study schooling and the ways in which ethnic studies in their schools are taken up, all the while striving to empower themselves as a community (see Cammarota, 2016; Cammarota & Fine, 2010). Currently, YPAR ethnic studies courses, although a small number when compared with ethnic studies as a whole, have taken root at the high school level. These projects teach students about research strategies and undergo research cycles, with the goal of solving community issues. The potential for these projects is transformed when ethnic studies itself, the classes students take, the impact it has, and the social activism needed to expand across districts become the object of investigation and a problem to be solved.

Third is research led by scholars as representatives of major institutions, which often produce data that policymakers listen to. The studies by

Cabrera and colleagues (2014) and Dee and Penner (2017) are examples that have played a vital role in institutionalized ethnic studies courses across the nation. But we also have outlined certain challenges with this approach. A major one is that academic institutions drive the research, even when it is designed at the service of communities or when partnerships with practitioners are seeded in collaborative ways. A major limitation is that this often leads to unsustainable projects that are dependent upon institutional funding or other resources.

Research is important to the future of ethnic studies, but it needs to be participatory, as discussed in this chapter. Ethnic studies contests the dominant vision of who we are as a nation, a vision that is rooted in European institutions and thought. Ethnic studies works toward a more inclusive democratic vision of who we are, one rooted in social justice and a value for the widely diverse ways of being human that constitute the nation and world. It is a given that ethnic studies will be resisted, particularly in today's anti-immigrant climate that is fueled in part by White nationalism, and exacerbated by media that become echo chambers for singular ideologies rather than venues for dialogue across differences. We believe it is important to engage children and youth from all different backgrounds in ethnic studies, in a way that speaks to their concerns without abandoning the hallmarks of ethnic studies. We believe it is crucial to engage with communities as part of that work, since historically disenfranchised communities stand up for movements that empower them, as does ethnic studies. We also see research as fundamentally important to improving and defending ethnic studies as we go forward, particularly research that is participatory as well as research that produces data that speak to policymakers. While policymakers may be strategically placed in the movement for ethnic studies, the potential for grassroots and participatory forms of research has yet to be investigated in the context of ethnic studies teaching and learning. We believe that articulating a "decolonizing" culturally responsive framework (Berryman, SooHoo, & Nevin, 2013; Smith, 2012; Zavala, 2013) can be useful as various communities and stakeholders seek ways to implement, enact, and reflect upon ethnic studies projects that are not just strategic but contextual and responsive to the needs of localized communities.

Moving forward, an important focal area for the movement is the development of ethnic studies at school or district levels nationally. The aforementioned research and advocacy point to expansion of ethnic studies on the basis that its projects are impactful, but where we need further reflection and intentional work is in the area of program design and development. Scaling up at school or district levels presents a series of generative problems, such as issues with institutionalization, schools as historically not serving students of color, entrenched ideologies, neoliberal attacks on public education, and so on.

But while these problems are quite present and palpable to students and teachers in the trenches, ethnic studies teaches us that there is always a movement forward, even amid these contradictions. It is these very conditions that can be transformed, through continued activism, contestation, and strategic community-building. It is these historical conditions that have persisted over the years but have themselves led to the necessity of ethnic studies as an expression of life, to what Bettina Love (2019) has termed *matterism*, the transition and struggle from survival to community development and self-determination.

References

Abeita, A., Chacon Díaz, L., Oemig, P., & Sleeter, C. (2016, April). *A critical literacy analysis of how non-mainstream ethnic groups are represented in public school textbooks*. Paper presented at the annual meeting of the American Educational Research Association, Chicago, IL.

Aboud, F. E., & Fenwick, V. (1999). Exploring and evaluating school-based interventions to reduce prejudice. *Journal of Social Issues, 55*(4), 767–786.

Aboud, F. E., Tredoux, C., Tropp, L. R., Brown, C. S., Niens, U., Noor, N. M., & Una Global Evaluation Group. (2012). Interventions to reduce prejudice and enhance inclusion and respect for ethnic differences in early childhood: A systematic review. *Developmental Review, 32*, 307–336.

Abu El-Haj, T. R. (2006). *Elusive justice: Wrestling with diversity and educational equity in everyday practice*. New York: Routledge.

Acosta, C. (2007). Developing critical consciousness: Resistance literature in a Chicano literature class. *English Journal, 97*(2), 36–42.

Acuña, R. (2007). *Occupied America: A history of Chicanos* (6th ed.). New York, NY: Pearson.

Adams, M., Bell, L. A., Goodman, D., & Joshi, K. Y. (Eds.). (2016). *Teaching for diversity and social justice* (3rd ed.). New York, NY: Routledge.

Adjapong, E. S., & Emdin, C. (2015). Rethinking pedagogy in urban spaces: Implementing hip-hop pedagogy in the urban science classroom. *Journal of Urban Learning Teaching and Research, 11*, 66–77.

Agarwal, R., Epstein, S., Oppenheim, R., Oyler, C., & Sonu, D. (2010). From ideal to practice and back again: Beginning teachers teaching for social justice. *Journal of Teacher Education, 61*(3), 237–247.

Agarwal-Rangnath, R. (2013). *Social studies, literacy, and social justice in the common core classroom: A guide for all teachers*. New York, NY: Teachers College Press.

Agarwal-Rangnath, R., Dover, A. G., & Henning, N. (2016). *Preparing to teach social studies for social justice: Becoming a renegade*. New York, NY: Teachers College Press.

Akom, A. A. (2009). Critical hip hop pedagogy as a form of liberatory praxis. *Equity & Excellence in Education, 42*(1), 52–66.

Akom, A. A., Cammarota, J., & Ginwright, S. (2008). Youthtopias: Towards a new paradigm of critical youth studies. *Youth Media Reporter, 2*(4), 1–30.

Alim, H. S., & Paris, D. (2017). What is culturally sustaining pedagogy and why does it matter? In D. Paris & H. S. Alim (Eds.), *Culturally sustaining pedagogies* (pp. 1–24). New York, NY: Teachers College Press.

Almarza, D. J., & Fehn, B. T. (1998). The construction of Whiteness in an American history classroom: A case study of eighth grade Mexican American students. *Transformations: The Journal of Inclusive Scholarship and Pedagogy, 9*(2), 196–211.

Alridge, D. P. (2006). The limits of master narratives in history textbooks. *Teachers College Record, 108*(4), 662–686.

Altschul, I., Oyserman, D., & Bybee, D. (2008). Racial-ethnic self-schemas and segmented assimilation: Identity and the academic achievement of Hispanic youth. *Social Psychology Quarterly, 71*(3), 302–320.

American Textbook Council. (2003). Islam and the textbooks: A report of the American Textbook Council. *Middle East Quarterly, 10*(3), 69ff.

Antonio, A. L., Chang, M. J., Hakuta, K., Kenny, D. A., Levin, S., & Milem, J. E. (2004). Effects of racial diversity on complex thinking in college students. *Psychological Science, 15*(8), 507–510.

Anyon, J. (1979). Ideology and United States history textbooks. *Harvard Educational Review, 49*(3), 361–386.

Apple, M. W. (2004). *Ideology and curriculum* (3rd ed.). New York, NY: Routledge Falmer.

Arce, M. S. (2016). Xicana/o indigenous epistemologies: Towards a decolonizing and liberatory education for Xicana/o youth. In D. Sandoval, A. Ratcliff, T. Buenavista, & J. R. Marín (Eds.), *Whitewashing American education: The new culture wars in ethnic studies* (Vol. 1, pp. 11–41). Santa Barbara, CA: Praeger.

Au, K. H. (1980). Participation structures in a reading lesson with Hawaiian children: Analysis of a culturally appropriate instructional event. *Anthropology & Education Quarterly, 11*(2), 91–115.

Au, K. H., & Carroll, J. H. (1997). Improving literacy achievement through a constructivist approach: The KEEP demonstration classroom project. *The Elementary School Journal, 97*(3), 203–221.

Au, W. (Ed.). (2009). *Rethinking multicultural education: Teaching for racial and cultural justice.* Milwaukee, WI: Rethinking Schools.

Au, W. (2012). The long march toward revitalization: Developing standpoint in curriculum studies. *Teachers College Record, 114*(5), 1–30.

Au, W., Brown, A. L., & Calderón, D. (2016). *Reclaiming the multicultural roots of U.S. curriculum.* New York, NY: Teachers College Press.

Ayers, W., Hunt, J. A., & Quinn, T. (Eds.). (1998). *Teaching for social justice. A democracy and education reader.* New York, NY: New Press.

Ayers, W., Quinn, T., & Stovall, D. (Eds.). (2009). *Handbook of social justice in education.* New York, NY: Routledge.

Bailey, C. T., & Boykin, A. W. (2001). The role of task variability and home contextual factors in the academic performance and task motivation of African American elementary school children. *Journal of Negro Education, 70* (1–2), 84–95.

Bakari, R. S. (1997). Epistemology from an Afrocentric perspective: Enhancing Black students' consciousness through an Afrocentric way of knowing. *Different Perspectives on Majority Rules, 20*. digitalcommons.unl.edu/pocpwi2/20

Ball, E. L., & Lai, A. (2006). Place-based pedagogy for the arts and humanities. *Pedagogy, 6*(2), 261–287.

Bang, M., Medin, D., Washinawatok, K., & Chapman, S. (2010). Innovations in culturally-based science education through partnerships and community. In M. Khine & I. Saleh (Eds.), *New science of learning: Cognition, computers and collaboration in education* (pp. 569–592). New York, NY: Springer.

Banks, J. A. (1993). The canon debate, knowledge construction, and multicultural education. *Educational Researcher, 22*(5), 4–140.

Banks, J. A. (1999). *An introduction to multicultural education* (2nd ed.). Boston, MA: Allyn & Bacon.

Banks, J. A. (2004). Race, knowledge construction, and education in the United States. In J. A. Banks & C.A.M. Banks (Eds.), *Handbook of research on multicultural education* (2nd ed., pp. 228–239). San Francisco, CA: Jossey-Bass.

Banks, J. A. (2008). *Teaching strategies for ethnic studies* (8th ed.). New York, NY: Pearson.

Baptiste, S. A. (2010). *Moving beyond Black history month: How three teachers interpreted and implemented the New Jersey Amistad legislation* (Unpublished doctoral dissertation). Rutgers University, New Brunswick, NJ.

Beaulieu, D. (2006). A survey and assessment of culturally based education programs for Native American students in the United States. *Journal of American Indian Education, 45*(2), 5–61.

Beckham, K., & Concordia, A. (2019). We don't want to just study the world, we want to change it. In R. T. Cuauhtin, M. Zavala, C. Sleeter, & W. Au (Eds.), *Rethinking ethnic studies* (pp. 319–327). Milwaukee, WI: Rethinking Schools.

Belgrave, F. Z., Chase-Vaughn, G., Gray, F., Addison, J. D., & Cherry, V. R. (2000). The effectiveness of a culture- and gender-specific intervention for increasing resiliency among African American preadolescent females. *Journal of Black Psychology, 26*(2), 133–147.

Berchini, C. (2016). Curriculum matters: Common core, authors of color, and inclusion for inclusion's sake. *Journal of Adolescent and Adult Literacy, 60* (1), 55–62.

Berryman, M., SooHoo, S., & Nevin, A. (2013). Culturally responsive methodologies from the margins. In M. Berryman, S. SooHoo, & A. Nevin (Eds.), *Culturally responsive methodologies* (pp. 1–34). Bingley, UK: Emerald.

Berta-Ávila, M. (2004). Critical Xicana/Xicano educators: Is it enough to be a person of color? *The High School Journal, 87*(4), 66–79.

Beyer, L., & Liston, D. (1996). *Curriculum in conflict*. New York, NY: Teachers College Press.

Bigler, R. S. (1999). The use of multicultural curricula and materials to counter racism in children. *Journal of Social Issues, 55*(4), 687–705.

Bigler, R. S., Brown, C. S., & Markell, M. (2001). When groups are not created equal: Effects of group status on the formation of intergroup attitudes in children. *Child Development, 72*, 1151–1162.

Boggs, G. (2012). *The next American revolution: Sustainable activism for the twenty-first century*. Berkeley, CA: University of California Press.

Bohman, J. (2005). Critical theory. *Stanford encyclopedia of philosophy*. plato.stanford.edu/archives/fall2008/entries/critical-theory/

Bower-Phipps, L., Cruz, M. C., Albaladejo, C., Johnson, A. M., & Homa, T. (2016). Emerging as teachers, as researchers, and as the "Other": A cooperative inquiry. *Networks: An Online Journal for Teacher Research, 18*(1). Retrieved from files. eric.ed.gov/fulltext/EJ1152312.pdf

Bowman, N. A. (2010a). College diversity experiences and cognitive development: A meta-analysis. *Review of Educational Research, 80*(1), 4–33.

Bowman, N. A. (2010b). Disequilibrium and resolution: The non-linear effects of diversity courses on well-being and orientations towards diversity. *The Review of Higher Education, 33*(4), 543–568.

Brown, A. L., & Brown, K. D. (2015). The more things change, the more they stay the same: Excavating race and the enduring racisms in U.S. curriculum. *Teachers College Record, 117*(14), 103–130.

Brown, D. L. (2017, June 7). When Portland banned Blacks: Oregon's shameful history as an "all-White" state. *The Washington Post*. Retrieved from washingtonpost.com

/news/retropolis/wp/2017/06/07/when-portland-banned-blacks-oregons-shameful -history-as-an-all-white-state/

Brown, K. D., & Brown, A. L. (2010). Silenced memories: An examination of the sociocultural knowledge on race and racial violence in official school curriculum. *Equity & Excellence in Education, 43*(2), 139–154.

Bruchac, J. (2003). *Our stories remember.* Golden, CO: Fulcrum.

Bruchac, J., & Locker, T. (1999). *Between Earth & sky: Legends of Native American sacred places.* San Diego, CA: Harcourt.

Brugar, K., Halvorsen, A. L., & Hernandez, S. (2014). Where are the women? A classroom inquiry into social studies textbooks. *Social Studies and the Young Learner, 26*(3), 28–31.

Busey, C. L., & Russell, W. B. (2017). "We want to learn": Middle school Latino/a students discuss social studies curriculum and pedagogy. *RMLE Online, 39*(4), 1–20.

Cabrera, N. L., Milam, J. F., Jaquette, O., & Marx, R. W. (2014). Missing the (student achievement) forest for all the (political) trees: Empiricism and the Mexican American student controversy in Tucson. *American Educational Research Journal, 51*(6), 1084–1118.

Cammarota, J. (2016). The praxis of ethnic studies: Transforming second sight into critical consciousness. *Race Ethnicity and Education, 19*(2), 233–251.

Cammarota, J., & Fine, M. (Eds.). (2010). *Revolutionizing education: Youth participatory action research in motion.* New York, NY: Routledge.

Cammarota, J., & Romero, A. (2009). The social justice education project: A critically compassionate intellectualism for Chicana/o students. In W. Ayers, T. Quinn, & D. Stovall (Eds.), *Handbook of social justice in education* (pp. 465–476). New York, NY: Routledge.

Campano, G., Ghiso, M. P., & Sánchez, L. (2013). "Nobody knows the . . . amount of a person": Elementary students critiquing dehumanization through organic critical literacies. *Research in the Teaching of English, 48*(1), 98–125.

Carjuzaa, J., Baldwin, A. E., & Munson, M. (2015). Making the dream real: Montana's Indian Education for All initiative thrives in a national climate of anti-ethnic studies. *Multicultural Perspectives, 17*(4), 198–206.

Cesar, S. (2011, November 20). Arizona educators clash over Mexican American studies. *LA Times.* Retrieved from articles.latimes.com/2011/nov/20/nation/la-na-ethnic -studies-20111120

Chang, M. J. (2002). The impact of an undergraduate diversity course requirement on students' racial views and attitudes. *The Journal of General Education, 51*(1), 21–42.

Chatterji, M. (2004). Evidence on "what works": An argument for extended-term mixed-method (ETMM) evaluation designs. *Educational Researcher, 33*(9), 3–13.

Chavous, T., Bernat, D. H., Schmeelk-Cone, K., Caldwell, C. H., Kohn-Wood, L., & Zimmerman, M. A. (2003). Racial identity and academic attainment among African American adolescents. *Child Development, 74*(4), 1076–1090.

Cherner, T., & Fegely, A. (2018). Answering Damarin's call: How iOS apps approach diversity, equity, and multiculturalism. *International Journal of Multicultural Education, 20*(1), 21–47.

Chick, K. A. (2006). Gender balance in K–12 American history textbooks. *Social Studies Research and Practice, 1*(3), 284–290.

Choi, Y., Lim, J. H., & An, S. (2011). Marginalized students' uneasy learning: Korean immigrant students' experiences of learning social studies. *Social Studies Research and Practice, 6*(3), 1–17.

Coburn, C. E., & Penuel, W. R. (2016). Research–practice partnerships in education: Outcomes, dynamics, and open questions. *Educational Researcher, 45*(1), 48–54.

Cole, M. (1998). *Cultural psychology: A once and future discipline.* Cambridge, MA: Harvard University Press.

Collins, P. H. (2002). *Black feminist thought: Knowledge, consciousness, and the politics of empowerment.* New York, NY: Routledge.

Copenhaver, J. (2001). Listening to their voices connect literary and cultural understandings: Responses to small group read-alouds of *Malcolm X: A Fire. New Advocate, 14*(4), 343–359.

Corntassel, J. (2012). Re-envisioning resurgence: Indigenous pathways to decolonization and sustainable self-determination. *Decolonization: Indigeneity, Education & Society, 1*(1), 86–101.

Crenshaw, K. (1989). Demarginalizing the intersection of race and sex: A Black feminist critique of antidiscrimination doctrine, feminist theory and antiracist politics. *University of Chicago Legal Forum, 1*(8), 139–167.

Crocco, M. S., & Costigan, A. T. (2007). The narrowing of curriculum and pedagogy in the age of accountability: Urban educators speak out. *Urban Education, 42*(6), 512–535.

Cuauhtin, R. T. (2019a). The ethnic studies framework: A holistic overview. In R. T. Cuauhtin, M. Zavala, C. Sleeter, & W. Au (Eds.), *Rethinking ethnic studies* (pp. 65–75). Milwaukee, WI: Rethinking Schools.

Cuauhtin, R. T. (2019b). Teaching John Bell's four I's of oppression. In In R. T. Cuauhtin, M. Zavala, C. Sleeter, & W. Au (Eds.), *Rethinking ethnic studies* (pp. 216–219). Milwaukee, WI: Rethinking Schools.

Cuauhtin, R. T., Zavala, M., Sleeter, C., & Au, W. (Eds.). (2019). *Rethinking ethnic studies.* Milwaukee, WI: Rethinking Schools.

Datnow, A. (2000). Power and politics in the adoption of school reform models. *Educational Evaluation and Policy Analysis, 22*(4), 357–374.

Daus-Magbual, R. R. (2010). *Political, emotional, powerful: The transformative influence of the Pin@y Educational Partnerships* (Unpublished doctoral dissertation). University of San Francisco, San Francisco, CA.

de los Rios, C. V. (2013). A curriculum of the borderlands: High school Chicana/o -Latina/o studies as sitios y lengua. *The Urban Review, 45*, 58–73.

de los Rios, C. V., López, J., & Morrell, E. (2015). Toward a critical pedagogy of race: Ethnic studies and literacies of power in high school classrooms. *Race and Social Problems, 7*, 84–96.

de los Ríos, C. V., López, J., & Morrell, E. (2016). Critical ethnic studies in high school classrooms: Academic achievement via social action. In P. A. Noguera, J. C. Pierce, & R. Ahram (Eds.), *Race, equity, and education* (pp. 177–198). New York, NY: Springer.

de los Ríos, C. V., & Ochoa, G. L. (2012). The people united shall never be divided: Reflections on community, collaboration, and change. *Journal of Latinos and Education, 11*, 271–279.

Dee, T., & Penner, E. (2017). The causal effects of cultural relevance: Evidence from an ethnic studies curriculum. *American Educational Research Journal, 54*(1), 127–166.

Delgado, R., & Stefancic, J. (2017). *Critical race theory: An introduction.* New York, NY: New York University Press.

DeMeulenaere, E. (2012). Toward a pedagogy of trust. In C. Dudley-Marling & S. Michaels (Eds.), *High-expectation curricula: Helping all students succeed with powerful learning* (pp. 28–41). New York, NY: Teachers College Press.

Denson, N. (2009). Do curricular and co-curricular activities influence racial bias? A meta-analysis. *Review of Educational Research, 79*(2), 805–838.

Derman-Sparks, L., & A. B. C. Task Force. (1989). *Anti-bias curriculum: Tools for empowering young children.* New York, NY: National Association for the Education of Young Children.

Diaz, E., & Flores, B. (2001). Teacher as sociocultural, sociohistorical mediator: Teaching to the potential. In M. Reyes & J. Halcón (Eds.), *The best for our children: Critical perspectives on literacy for Latino students* (pp. 29–47). New York, NY: Teachers College Press.

Doherty, R. W., & Hilberg, R. S. (2007). Standards for effective pedagogy, classroom organization, English proficiency, and student achievement. *The Journal of Educational Research, 101*(1), 23–34.

Doherty, R. W., Hilberg, R. S., Pinal, A., & Tharp, R. G. (2003). Five standards and student achievement. *NABE Journal of Research and Practice, 1*(1), 1–24.

Dover, A. G. (2013). Teaching for social justice: From conceptual frameworks to classroom practices. *Multicultural Perspectives, 15*(1), 3–11.

Dudgeon, P., & Fielder, J. (2006). Third spaces within tertiary places: Indigenous Australian studies. *Journal of Community and Applied Social Psychology, 16*, 396–409.

Duncan, W. (2012). The effects of Africentric United States history curriculum on Black student achievement. *Contemporary Issues in Education Research, 5*(2), 91–96.

Duncan-Andrade, J.M.R., & Morrell, E. (2008). *The art of critical pedagogy.* New York, NY: Peter Lang.

Eigenberg, H. M., & Park, S. M. (2016). Marginalization and invisibility of women of color: A content analysis of race and gender images in introductory criminal justice and criminology texts. *Race and Justice, 6*(3), 257–279.

Elia, N., Hernández, D. M., Kim, J., Redmond, S. L., Rodríguez, D., & See, S. E. (Eds.). (2016). *Critical ethnic studies: A reader.* Durham, NC: Duke University Press.

Engberg, M. E. (2004). Improving intergroup relations in higher education: A critical examination of the influence of educational interventions on racial bias. *Review of Educational Research, 74*(4), 473–524.

Engeström, Y. (2011). From design experiments to formative interventions. *Theory & Psychology, 21*(5), 598–628.

Epstein, T. (2001). Racial identity and young people's perspectives on social education. *Theory Into Practice, 40*(1), 42–47.

Epstein, T. (2009). *Interpreting national history.* New York, NY: Routledge.

Eraqi, M. M. (2015). Inclusion of Arab-Americans and Muslim-Americans within secondary U.S. history textbooks. *Journal of International Social Studies, 5*(1), 64–80.

Espinoza, M. L., & Vossoughi, S. (2014). Perceiving learning anew: Social interaction, dignity, and educational rights. *Harvard Educational Review, 84*(3), 285–313.

Faircloth, S. C. (2015). The early childhood education of American Indian and Alaska Native children: State of the research. *Journal of American Indian Education, 54*(1), 99–126.

Few-Demo, A. L. (2014). Intersectionality as the "new" critical approach in feminist family studies. *Journal of Family Theory and Review, 6*, 168–183.

Ford, D. Y., & Harris, J. J., III. (2000). A framework for infusing multicultural curriculum into gifted education. *Roeper Review, 23*(1), 4–10.

Forest, D.E.F., Garrison, K.L.G., & Kimmel, S.C.C. (2015). "The university for the poor": Portrayals of class in translated children's literature. *Teachers College Record, 117*(2), 1–40.

Freire, P. (2000). *Pedagogy of freedom: Ethics, democracy, and civic courage*. Lanham, MD: Rowman & Littlefield.

Fusarelli, L. D. (2008). Flying (partially) blind: School leaders' use of research in decision making. *Phi Delta Kappan, 89*(5), 365–368.

Galeano, E. (1997). *Open veins of Latin America: Five centuries of the pillage of a continent*. New York, NY: Monthly Review Press.

Gay, G. (1983). Multiethnic education: Historical developments and future prospects. *Phi Delta Kappan, 64*, 560–563.

Gay, G. (2018). *Culturally responsive teaching* (3rd ed.). New York, NY: Teachers College Press.

Ginwright, S. A. (2000). Identity for sale: The limits of racial reform in urban schools. *The Urban Review, 32*(1), 87–104.

Ginwright, S. (2004). *Black in school: Afrocentric reform, urban youth, and the promise of hip-hop culture*. New York, NY: Teachers College Press.

Gómez, L. G. (2007). *Manifest destinies: The making of the Mexican American race*. New York, NY: New York University Press.

González, N., Moll, L. C., & Amanti, C. (Eds.). (2005). *Funds of knowledge: Theorizing practices in households, communities, and classrooms*. Mahwah, NJ: Erlbaum.

González, R. A., Rosendo-Servín, M., & Williams, D. A. (2019). The struggle for ethnic studies in the golden state: Capitol city organizers and activists. In R. T. Cuauhtin, M. Zavala, C. Sleeter, & W. Au (Eds.), *Rethinking ethnic studies* (pp. 308–314). Milwaukee, WI: Rethinking Schools.

Grant, C. A., & Sleeter, C. E. (2009). *Turning on learning* (5th ed.). Hoboken, NJ: Wiley.

Green-Gibson, A., & Collett, A. (2014). A comparison of African & mainstream culture on African American students in public elementary schools. *Multicultural Education, 21*(2), 33–37.

Grosfoguel, R. (2012). The dilemmas of ethnic studies in the United States: Between liberal multiculturalism, identity politics, disciplinary colonization, and decolonial epistemologies. *Human Architecture: Journal of the Sociology of Self-Knowledge, 10*(1), 81–90.

Grossman, P., & Thompson, C. (2008). Learning from curriculum materials: Scaffolds for new teachers? *Teaching and Teacher Education, 24*(8), 2014–2026.

Gruenewald, D. A. (2003). The best of both worlds: A critical pedagogy of place. *Educational Researcher, 32*(4), 3–12.

Gurin, P. Y., Dey, E. L., Gurin, G., & Hurtado, S. (2003). How does racial/ethnic diversity promote education? *The Western Journal of Black Studies, 27*(1), 20–29.

Gurin, P. Y., Dey, E. L., Hurtado, S., & Gurin, G. (2002). Diversity and higher education: Theory and impact on educational outcomes. *Harvard Educational Review, 72*(3), 330–367.

Gurin, P., & Nagda, B.R.A. (2006). Getting to the what, how, and why of diversity on campus. *Educational Researcher, 35*(1), 20–24.

Gyasi, Y. (2016). *Homegoing*. New York, NY: Knopf.

Halagao, P. E. (2004). Holding up the mirror: The complexity of seeing your ethnic self in history. *Theory and Research in Social Education, 32*(4), 459–483.

Halagao, P. E. (2010). Liberating Filipino Americans through decolonizing curriculum. *Race Ethnicity & Education, 13*(4), 495–512.

Hale-Benson, J. (1990). Visions for children: African American early childhood education program. *Early Childhood Research Quarterly, 5*(2), 199–213.

Hall, T., & Martin, B. (2013). Engagement of African American college students through the use of hip-hop pedagogy. *International Journal of Pedagogies and Learning, 8*(2), 93–105.

Harding, S. G. (Ed.). (2004). *The feminist standpoint theory reader: Intellectual and political controversies.* New York, NY: Routledge.

Hayes, C., & Juarez, B. (2012). There is no culturally responsive teaching spoken here: A critical race perspective. *Democracy and Education, 20*(1), 1–14.

Heilig, J. V., Brown, K. D., & Brown, A. L. (2012). The illusion of inclusion: A critical race theory textual analysis of race and standards. *Harvard Educational Review, 82*(3), 403–424.

Hilberg, R. S., Tharp, R. G., & DeGeest, L. (2000). The efficacy of CREDE standards-based instruction on American Indian mathematics classes. *Excellence & Equity in Education, 33*(2), 32–40.

Hogan, D. E., & Mallott, M. (2005). Changing racial prejudice through diversity education. *Journal of College Student Development, 46*(2), 115–125.

Hogben, M., & Waterman, C. K. (1997). Are all of your students represented in their textbooks? A content analysis of coverage of diversity issues in introductory psychology textbooks. *Teaching of Psychology, 24*(2), 95–100.

hooks, b. (1989). Choosing the margin as a space of radical openness. *Framework: The Journal of Cinema and Media,* No. 36, 15–23.

Hu-DeHart, E. (2004). Ethnic studies in U.S. higher education: History, development, and goals. In J. A. Banks & C.A.M. Banks (Eds.), *Handbook of research on multicultural education* (2nd ed., pp. 869–881). San Francisco, CA: Jossey-Bass.

Hughes, J. M., Bigler, R. S., & Levy, S. R. (2007). Consequences of learning about historical racism among European American and African American children. *Child Development, 78,* 1689–1705.

Hughes, R. L. (2007). A hint of Whiteness: History textbooks and social construction of race in the wake of the sixties. *The Social Studies, 98*(5), 201–207.

Husband, T. (2010). He's too young to learn about that stuff: Anti-racist pedagogy and early childhood social studies. *Social Studies Research & Practice, 5*(2), 61–75.

Ihimaera, W. (2005). *The whale rider.* Portsmouth, NH: Heinemann.

Irizarry, J. G. (2009). Reinvigorating multicultural education through youth participatory action research. *Multicultural Perspectives, 11*(4), 194–199.

Janks, H. (2017). *Doing critical literacy: Texts and activities for students and teachers.* New York, NY: Routledge.

John-Steiner, V., & Mahn, H. (1996). Sociocultural approaches to learning and development: A Vygotskian framework. *Educational Psychologist, 31*(3–4), 191–206.

Johnson, R. B., & Onwuegbuzie, A. J. (2004). Mixed methods research: A research paradigm whose time has come. *Educational Researcher, 33*(7), 14–26.

Jojola, T., Lee, T. S., & Alcántara, A. N. (2011). *Indian education in New Mexico 2025.* Santa Fe, NM: New Mexico Public Education Department, Indian Education Division.

Jupp, J. C. (2013). *Becoming teachers of inner-city students: Life histories and teacher stories of committed White teachers.* Boston, MA: Sense Publishers.

Jupp, J. C. (2017). What learning is needed for White teachers' race-visible teaching? Racialised curriculum recoding of cherished knowledges. *Whiteness and Education, 2*(1), 15–31. doi:10.1080/23793406.2017.1373032

Kailin, J. (2002). *Antiracist education: From theory to practice.* New York, NY: Rowman & Littlefield.

Kaufmann, D., Johnson, S. M., Kardos, S. M., Liu, E., & Peske, H. G. (2002). "Lost at sea": New teachers' experiences with curriculum and assessment. *Teachers College Record, 104*(2), 273–300.

Kelley, J. E., & Darragh, J. J. (2011). Depictions and gaps: Portrayal of U.S. poverty in realistic fiction children's picture books. *Reading Horizons, 50*(4), 263–282.

King, J. E. (Ed.). (2005). *Black education: A transformative research and action agenda for the new century*. New York, NY: Routledge & Washington, DC: American Educational Research Association.

King, L. J. (2014). When lions write history. *Multicultural Education, 22*(1), 2–11.

King, L. J. (2017). The status of Black history in U.S. schools and society. *Social Education, 81*(1), 14–18.

King, L. J., & Brown, K. (2014). Once a year to be Black: Fighting against typical Black history month pedagogies. *The Negro Educational Review, 65*(1–4), 23–43.

Kisker, E. E., Lipka, J., Adams, B. L., Rickard, A., Andrew-Ihrke, D., Yanez, E. E., & Millard, A. (2012). The potential of a culturally based supplemental mathematics curriculum to improve the mathematics performance of Alaska Native and other students. *Journal for Research in Mathematics Education, 43*(1), 75–113.

Kivel, P. (2013). *Living in the shadow of the cross*. Gabriola Island, BC: New Society Publishers.

Klepper, A. (2014). High school students' attitudes toward Islam and Muslims: Can a social studies course make a difference? *The Social Studies, 105*, 113–123.

Krater, J., & Zeni, J. (1995). Seeing students, seeing culture, seeing ourselves. *Voices from the Middle, 3*(3), 32–38.

Krater, J., Zeni, J., & Cason, N. D. (1994). *Mirror images: Teaching writing in Black and White*. Portsmouth, NH: Heinemann.

Kumashiro, K. (2000). Toward a theory of anti-oppressive education. *Review of Educational Research, 70*(1), 25–53.

Ladson-Billings, G. (1992). Culturally relevant teaching: The key to making multicultural education work. In C. A. Grant (Ed.), *Research and multicultural education: From the margins to the mainstream* (pp. 106–121). Washington, DC: Falmer Press.

Ladson-Billings, G. (1995). Toward a theory of culturally relevant pedagogy. *American Educational Research Journal, 32*(3), 465–491.

Lareau, A. (2009). Narrow questions, narrow answers: The limited value of randomized controlled trials for education research. In P. Walters, A. Lareau, & S. Ranis (Eds.), *Education research on trial: Policy reform and the call for scientific rigor* (pp. 155–172). New York, NY: Routledge.

Lee, C. D. (1995). A culturally based cognitive apprenticeship: Teaching African American high school students skills in literary interpretation. *Reading Research Quarterly, 30*(4), 608–630.

Lee, C. D. (2001). Is October Brown Chinese? A cultural modeling activity system for underachieving students. *American Educational Research Journal, 38*(1), 97–142.

Lee, C. D. (2006). "Every good-bye ain't gone": Analyzing the cultural underpinnings of classroom talk. *International Journal of Qualitative Studies in Education, 19*(3), 305–327.

Lee, C. D. (2007). *Culture, literacy, and learning: Taking bloom in the midst of the whirlwind*. New York, NY: Teachers College Press.

Lee, T. S., & Quijada Cerecer, P. D. (2010). (Re)claiming Native youth knowledge: Engaging in socio-culturally responsive teaching and relationships. *Multicultural Perspectives, 12*(4), 199–205.

Leistyna, P. (2004). Presence of mind in the process of learning and knowing: A dialogue with Paulo Freire. *Teacher Education Quarterly, 31*(1), 17–30.

Lewis, K. M., Andrews, E., Gaska, K., Sullivan, C., Bybee, D., & Ellick, K. L. (2012). Experimentally evaluating the impact of a school-based African-centered emancipatory intervention on the ethnic identity of African American adolescents. *Journal of Black Psychology, 38*(3), 259–289.

Lewis, K. M., Sullivan, C. M., & Bybee, D. (2006). An experimental evaluation of a school-based emancipatory intervention to promote African American well-being and youth leadership. *Journal of Black Psychology, 32*(1), 3–28.

Liou, D. D., Martinez, A. N., & Rotheram-Fuller, E. (2016). "Don't give up on me": Critical mentoring pedagogy for the classroom building students' community cultural wealth. *International Journal of Qualitative Studies in Education, 29*(1), 104–129.

Lipka, J., Hogan, M. P., Webster, J. P., Yanez, E., Adams, B., Clark, S., & Lacy, D. (2005). Math in a cultural context: Two case studies of a successful culturally-based math project. *Anthropology & Education Quarterly, 36*(4), 367–385.

López, F. A. (2016). Culturally responsive pedagogies in Arizona and Latino students' achievement. *Teachers College Record, 118*(5), 1–42.

López, F. A. (2017). Altering the trajectory of the self-fulfilling prophecy: Asset-based pedagogy and classroom dynamics. *Journal of Teacher Education, 68*(2), 193–212.

López, F. A. (2018). *Asset pedagogies in Latino youth identity and achievement.* New York, NY: Routledge.

Lopez, G. E. (2004). Interethnic contact, curriculum, and attitudes in the first year of college. *Journal of Social Issues, 40*(1), 75–94.

López, N. (2008). Antiracist pedagogy and empowerment in a bilingual classroom in the U.S., circa 2006. *Theory Into Practice, 47*(1), 43–50.

Love, B. L. (2014). Urban storytelling: How storyboarding, moviemaking, and hip-hop-based education can promote students' critical voice. *English Journal, 103*(5), 53–58.

Love, B. (2019). *We want to do more than survive: Abolitionist teaching and the pursuit of educational freedom.* Boston, MA: Beacon Press.

Low, J. T. (2013). Why hasn't the number of multicultural books increased in eighteen years? The Open Book blog. Lee & Low Books. Retrieved from blog.leeandlow.com/2013/06/17/why-hasnt-the-number-of-multicultural-books-increased-in-eighteen-years

Luke, A. (1991). Literacies as social practices. *English Education, 23*(3), 131–147.

Lynn, M. (1999). Toward a critical race pedagogy: A research note. *Urban Education, 33*(5), 606–626.

Mack, L. (2010). The philosophical underpinnings of educational research. *Pollyglossia, 19*(1), 5–11.

Mahiri, J. (2017). *Deconstructing race.* New York, NY: Teachers College Press.

Martin, K. J. (2010). Student attitudes and the teaching and learning of race, culture and politics. *Teaching and Teacher Education, 26*(3), 530–539.

Martinez, G. (2010). *Native pride.* Cresskill, NJ: Hampton Press.

Marx, S. (2008). Popular White teachers of Latina/o kids. *Urban Education, 43*(1), 29–67.

Matthews, C. E., & Smith, W. S. (1994). Native American related materials in elementary science instruction. *Journal of Research in Science Teaching, 31*(4), 363–380.

Maxwell, J. A. (2004). Causal explanation, qualitative research, and scientific inquiry in education. *Educational Researcher, 33*(2), 3–11.

May, S., & Sleeter, C. E. (Eds.). (2010). *Critical multiculturalism: Theory and praxis.* New York, NY: Routledge.

McCall, L. (2005). The complexity of intersectionality. *Signs: Journal of Women and Culture in Society, 30*(3), 1771–1800.

McCarty, T. L. (1993). Language, literacy, and the image of the child in American Indian classrooms. *Language Arts, 70*(3), 182–192.

McCarty, T. L., & Lee, T. S. (2014). Critical culturally sustaining/revitalizing pedagogy and Indigenous education sovereignty. *Harvard Educational Review, 84*(1), 101–124.

McNair, J. C. (2003). It really is the little things! More thoughts about the insider/outsider debate. *The New Advocate, 16*, 129–138.

Mignolo, W. D. (2007). Delinking: The rhetoric of modernity, the logic of coloniality and the grammar of de-coloniality. *Cultural Studies, 21*(2–3), 449–514.

Mignolo, W. D. (2012). *Local histories/global designs: Coloniality, subaltern knowledges, and border thinking.* Princeton, NJ: Princeton University Press.

Mitchell, D. E. (1980). The ideological factor in school politics. *Education and Urban Society, 12*(4), 436–451.

Mora, J., & Diaz, D. (2014). *Latino social policy: A participatory research model.* New York, NY: Routledge.

Morrell, E. (2015). *Critical literacy and urban youth: Pedagogies of access, dissent, and liberation.* New York, NY: Routledge.

Mudimbe, V. Y. (1988). *The invention of Africa: Gnosis, philosophy, and the order of knowledge.* Bloomington, IN: Indiana University Press.

Nagda, B. A., Kim, C. W., & Truelove, Y. (2004). Learning about difference, learning with others, learning to transgress. *Journal of Social Issues, 60*(1), 195–214.

Navarro, O. (2018). We can't do this alone: Validating and inspiring social justice teaching through a community of transformative praxis. *Curriculum Inquiry, 48*(3), 335–358.

Neuliep, J. W. (2008). *Intercultural communication: A contextual approach.* Thousand Oaks, CA: Sage.

Neville, H. A., Poteat, V. P., Lewis, J. A., & Spanierman, L. B. (2014). Changes in White college students' color-blind racial ideology over 4 years: Do diversity experiences make a difference? *Journal of Counseling Psychology, 61*(2), 179–190.

Newcomer, S. N. (2018). Investigating the power of authentically caring student–teacher relationships for Latinx students. *Journal of Latinos and Education, 17*(2), 179–193.

Newman, F. (2012). *Teacher resources for an African-centered/global education curriculum in early childhood education.* Retrieved from snlapps.depaul.edu/writing/NewmanAPproduct2012.pdf

Noboa, J. (2005). *Leaving Latinos out of history: Teaching U.S. history in Texas.* New York, NY: Routledge.

Ochoa, G. L. (2007). *Learning from Latino teachers.* San Francisco, CA: Jossey-Bass.

Okoye-Johnson, O. (2011). Does multicultural education improve students' racial attitudes? Implications for closing the achievement gap. *Journal of Black Studies, 42*(8), 1252–1274.

Olivio, C. (2012). Bringing women in: Gender and American government and politics textbooks. *Journal of Political Science Education, 8*(2), 131–146.

Paone, T. R., Malott, K. M., & Barr, J. J. (2015). Assessing the impact of a race-based course on counseling students: A quantitative study. *Journal of Multicultural Counseling and Development, 43*, 206–220.

Paris, D., & Alim, H. S. (Eds.). (2017). *Culturally sustaining pedagogies: Teaching and learning for justice in a changing world.* New York, NY: Teachers College Press.

Pelligrino, A., Mann, L., & Russell, W. B., III. (2013). Lift as we climb: A textbook analysis of the segregated school experience. *The High School Journal, 96*(3), 209–231.

Perry, T., Steele, C., & Hilliard, A., III. (2003). *Young, gifted and Black.* Boston, MA: Beacon Press.

Philip, T., & Zavala, M. (2016). The possibilities of being "critical": Discourses that limit options for educators of color. *Urban Education, 51*(6), 659–682.

Piatek-Jimenez, K., Madison, M., & Przybyla-Kucheck, J. (2014). Equity in mathematics textbooks: A new look at an old issue. *Journal of Women and Minorities in Science and Engineering, 20*(1), 55–74.

Picower, B. (2009). The unexamined Whiteness of teaching: How White teachers maintain and enact dominant racial ideologies. *Race Ethnicity and Education, 12*(2), 197–215.

Picower, B. (2012). *Practice what you teach: Social justice education in the classroom and the streets.* New York, NY: Routledge.

Quijano, A. (2007). Coloniality and modernity/rationality. *Cultural Studies, 21*(2–3), 168–178.

Rangel, J. (2007). The educational legacy of *El Plan de Santa Barbara*: An interview with Reynaldo Macías. *Journal of Latinos and Education, 6*(2), 191–199.

Raudenbush, S. W. (2005). Learning from attempts to improve schooling: The contribution of methodological diversity. *Educational Researcher, 34*(5), 25–31.

Reese, D. (2007). Proceed with caution: Using Native American folktales in the classroom. *Language Arts, 84*(3), 245–256.

Rickford, A. (2001). The effect of cultural congruence and higher order questioning on the reading enjoyment and comprehension of ethnic minority students. *Journal of Education for Students Placed at Risk, 6*(4), 357–387.

Rocco, T. S., Bernier, J. D., & Bowman, L. (2014). Critical race theory and HRD: Moving race front and center. *Advances in Developing Human Resources, 16*(4), 457–470.

Rogoff, B. (2003). *The cultural nature of human development.* New York, NY: Oxford University Press.

Rojas, M. A. (2010). (Re)visioning U.S. Latino literatures in high school English classrooms. *English Education, 42*(3), 263–277.

Saleem, M. M., & Thomas, M. K. (2011). The reporting of the September 11th terrorist attacks in American social studies textbooks: A Muslim perspective. *The High School Journal, 95*(1), 15–33.

San Pedro, T. (2018a). Abby as ally: An argument for culturally disruptive pedagogy. *American Educational Research Journal, 55*(6), 1193–1232.

San Pedro, T. (2018b). Sustaining ourselves in unsustainable places: Revitalizing sacred landscapes within schools. *Journal of Adolescent and Adult Literacy, 62*(3), 333–336.

San Pedro, T., & Kinloch, V. (2017). Toward projects in humanization: Research on co-creating and sustaining dialogic relationships. *American Educational Research Journal, 54*(1), 373–394.

Sanchez, T. R. (2007). The depiction of Native Americans in recent (1991–2004) secondary American history textbooks: How far have we come? *Equity & Excellence in Education, 40*, 311–320.

Sanders, F. C. (2009). *A curricular policy forty years in the making: The implementation of an African American history course in the Philadelphia school district* (Unpublished doctoral dissertation). Pennsylvania State University, University Park, PA.

Schocker, J. B., & Woyshner, C. (2013). Representing African American women in U.S. history textbooks. *The Social Studies, 103*, 32–31.

Sharif Matthews, J., & López, F. (2018). Speaking their language: The role of cultural content integration and heritage language for academic achievement among Latino children. *Contemporary Educational Psychology, 57*, 72–86.

Skerrett, A. (2011). English teachers' racial literacy knowledge and practice. *Race Ethnicity and Education, 14*(3), 313–330.

Slavin, R. E. (2005). Evidence-based reform in education: Promise and pitfalls. *Mid-Western Educational Researcher, 18*(1), 8–13.

Sleeter, C. E. (2000). Creating an empowering multicultural curriculum. *Race, Gender & Class, 7*(3), 178–196.

Sleeter, C. E. (2001). Preparing teachers for culturally diverse schools: Research and the overwhelming presence of Whiteness. *Journal of Teacher Education, 52*(2), 94–106.

Sleeter, C. E. (2011). *The academic and social value of ethnic studies: A research review.* Washington, DC: National Education Association.

Sleeter, C. E. (2016). Multicultural programming in New Mexico. Expert witness report to MALDEF prepared for *Martinez v. New Mexico,* D-101-CV-2014-00793.

Sleeter, C. E., & Cornbleth, C. (Eds.). (2011). *Teaching with vision: Culturally responsive teaching in standards-based classrooms.* New York, NY: Teachers College Press.

Sleeter, C. E., & Delgado Bernal, D. (2004). Critical pedagogy, critical race theory, and antiracist education: Implications for multicultural education. In J. A. Banks & C.A.M. Banks (Eds.), *Handbook of research on multicultural education* (2nd ed., pp. 240–258). San Francisco, CA: Jossey-Bass.

Sleeter, C. E., & Grant, C. A. (1991). Textbooks and race, class, gender and disability. In M. W. Apple & L. Christian-Smith (Eds.), *Politics of the textbook* (pp. 78–110). New York, NY: Routledge, Chapman and Hall.

Smith, L. T. (2012). *Decolonizing methodologies: Research and Indigenous peoples.* New York, NY: Zed Books.

Smith, L. T., Tuck, E., & Yang, K. W. (Eds.). (2018). *Indigenous and decolonizing studies in education: Mapping the long view.* New York, NY: Routledge.

Smolkin, L. B., & Young, C. A. (2011). Missing mirrors, missing windows: Children's literature textbooks and LGBT topics. *Language Arts, 88*(3), 217–225.

Sosniak, L. A., & Stodolsky, S. S. (1993). Teachers and textbooks: Materials used in fourth-grade classrooms. *The Elementary School Journal, 93*(3), 249–275.

Southern Poverty Law Center. (2018). *Teaching hard history: American slavery.* Montgomery, AL: Author.

Souto-Manning, M., & Rabadi-Raol, A. (2018). (Re)centering quality in early childhood education: Toward intersectional justice for minoritized children. *Review of Research in Education, 42,* 203–225.

Spanierman, L. B., & Heppner, M. J. (2004). Psychosocial costs of racism to Whites scale (PCRW): Construction and initial validation. *Journal of Counseling Psychology, 51*(2), 249–262.

Speed, S. (2017). Structures of settler capitalism in Abya Yala. *American Quarterly, 69*(4), 783–790.

Spring, J. (2016). *Deculturalization and the struggle for equity: A brief history of the education of dominated cultures in the United States* (2nd ed.). New York, NY: McGraw-Hill.

Stanton, C. R. (2014). The curricular Indian agent: Discursive colonization and Indigenous (dys)agency in U.S. history textbooks. *Curriculum Inquiry, 44*(5), 649–676.

Stanton, C. R., & Morrison, D. (2018). Investigating curricular policy as a tool to dismantle the master's house: Indian Education for All and social studies teacher education. *Policy Futures in Education, 16*(6), 729–748.

Stone, B. J., & Stewart, S. (2016). HBCUs and writing programs: Critical hip hop language pedagogy and first-year student success. *Composition Studies, 44*(2), 183–186.

Swartz, E. (2009). Diversity: Gatekeeping knowledge and maintaining inequalities. *Review of Educational Research, 79*(2), 1044–1083.

Takagi, D. (2015). First precepts for democracy and research practices in ethnic studies: Iteration, collaboration, and reflection. *Cultural Studies Critical Methodologies, 15*(2), 100–111.

Teaching Tolerance. (2014). *Critical practices for anti-bias education.* Retrieved from tolerance.org/sites/default/files/Critical%20Practicesv4_final.pdf

Terzian, S. G., & Yaeger, E. A. (2007). "That's when we became a nation": Urban Latino adolescents and the designation of historical significance. *Urban Education, 42*(1), 52–81.

Tharp, R. G., & Gallimore, R. (1988). *Rousing minds to life: Teaching, learning, and schooling in social context.* Cambridge, UK: Cambridge University Press.

Thomas, O., Davidson, W., & McAdoo, H. (2008). An evaluation study of the Young Empowered Sisters (YES!) Program: Promoting cultural assets among African American adolescent girls through a culturally relevant school-based intervention. *Journal of Black Psychology, 34*(3), 281–308.

Thompson, N. L., Hare, D., Sempier, T. T., & Grace, C. (2008). The development of a curriculum toolkit with America Indian and Alaska Native communities. *Early Childhood Education, 35,* 397–404.

Thornhill, T. E. (2016). Resistance and assent: How racial socialization shapes Black students' experience learning African American history in high school. *Urban Education, 51*(9) 1126–1151.

Tingle, T. (2013). *How I became a ghost.* Oklahoma City, OK: Roadrunner Press.

Tintiangco-Cubales, A., Daus-Magbual, A., Desai, M., Sabac, A., & Torres, M. V. (2016). Into our hoods: Where critical performance pedagogy births resistance. *International Journal of Qualitative Studies in Education, 29*(10), 1308–1325.

Tintiangco-Cubales, A., Kohli, R., Sacramento, J., Henning, N., Agarwal-Rangnath, R., & Sleeter, C. (2015). Toward an ethnic studies pedagogy: Implications for K–12 schools from the research. *The Urban Review, 47*(1), 104–125.

Todd, N. R., Spanierman, L. B., & Poteat, V. P. (2011). Longitudinal examination of the psychosocial costs of racism to Whites across the college experience. *Journal of Counseling Psychology, 58*(4), 508–521.

Tyson, C. A. (2002). "Get up off that thing": African American middle school students respond to literature to develop a framework for understanding social action. *Theory and Research in Social Education, 30*(1), 42–65.

Valdez, C. (2018). Flippin' the scripted curriculum: Ethnic studies inquiry in elementary education. *Race Ethnicity and Education.* doi.org/10.1080/13613324.2018 .1497959

Valenzuela, A. (2010). *Subtractive schooling: U.S.-Mexican youth and the politics of caring.* New York, NY: State University of New York Press.

Valli, L., Croninger, R. G., Chambliss, M. J., Graeber, A. O., & Buese, D. (2008). *Test driven: High stakes accountability in elementary schools.* New York, NY: Teachers College Press.

Vasquez, J. M. (2005). Ethnic identity and Chicano literature: How ethnicity affects reading and reading affects ethnic consciousness. *Ethnic and Racial Studies, 28*(5), 903–924.

Vasquez, R. L., & Altschuler, D. (2017). A critical examination of K–12 ethnic studies: Transforming and liberating praxis. *Journal of Critical Thought and Praxis, 6*(2), 22–41.

Vaught, S. E., & Castagno, A. E. (2008). "I don't think I'm a racist": Critical race theory, teacher attitudes, and structural racism. *Race Ethnicity and Education, 11*(2), 95–113.

Wallis, V. (1997). *Bird girl and the man who followed the sun.* New York, NY: Harper Perennial.

Watkins, W. (1993). Black curriculum orientations: A preliminary inquiry. *Harvard Educational Review, 63*(3), 321–338.

White, K., Rumsey, S. K., & Stevens, A. (2016). Are we "there" yet? The treatment of gender and feminism in technical, business, and workplace writing studies. *Journal of Technical Writing and Communication, 46*(1), 27–58.

Wiggan, G. (2007). From opposition to engagement: Lessons from high achieving African American students. *The Urban Review, 40*(4), 317–349.

Wiggan, G., & Watson-Vandiver, M. J. (2017). Pedagogy of empowerment: Student perspectives on critical multicultural education at a high-performing African American school. *Race Ethnicity and Education, 22*(6), 767–787.

Wiggins, G., & McTighe, J. (2005). *Understanding by design* (2nd ed.). New York, NY: Pearson.

Woodson, A. N. (2015). "What you supposed to know": Urban Black students' perspectives on history textbooks. *Journal of Urban Learning Teaching and Research, 11*, 57–65.

Woodson, A. N. (2017). "There ain't no White people here": Master narratives of the civil rights movement in the stories of urban youth. *Urban Education, 52*(3), 316–342.

Yosso, T. J. (2002). Toward a critical race curriculum. *Equity & Excellence in Education, 35*(2), 93–107.

Yosso, T. J. (2005). Whose culture has capital? A critical race theory discussion of community cultural wealth. *Race Ethnicity and Education, 8*(1), 69–91. doi.org/10 .1080/1361332052000341006

Zakin, A. (2012). Hand to hand: Teaching tolerance and social justice one child at a time. *Childhood Education, 88*(1), 3–13.

Zavala, M. (2013). What do we mean by decolonizing research strategies? Lessons from decolonizing, Indigenous research projects in New Zealand and Latin America. *Decolonization: Indigeneity, Education & Society, 2*(1), 55–71.

Zavala, M. (2019a). Decolonial literacies, mediation, and critical consciousness. In *Raza struggle and the movement for ethnic studies: Decolonial pedagogies, literacies, and methodologies* (pp. 101–140). New York, NY: Peter Lang.

Zavala, M. (2019b). *Raza struggle and the movement for ethnic studies: Decolonial pedagogies, literacies, and methodologies.* New York, NY: Peter Lang.

Zeichner, K. M. (1995). Beyond the divide of teacher research and academic research. *Teachers and Teaching, 1*(2), 153–172.

Index

About the Authors

Christine E. Sleeter, PhD., is professor emerita in the College of Education at California State University, Monterey Bay, where she was a founding faculty member. She has served as a visiting professor at several universities, including the University of Maine, University of Colorado Boulder, Victoria University of Wellington and the University of Auckland in New Zealand, and Universidad Nacional de Educación a Distancia in Madrid, Spain. She is past president of the National Association for Multicultural Education, and past vice president of the American Educational Research Association. Her research focuses on anti-racist multicultural education, ethnic studies, and teacher education. She has published over 150 articles and 23 books, including *Un-Standardizing Curriculum* (2nd ed. with J. Flores Carmona, Teachers College Press) and *Rethinking Ethnic Studies* (with R. T. Cuauhtin, M. Zavala, & W. Au); she has also published two novels that feature teachers as main characters (*White Bread* and *The Inheritance*). Awards for her work include the American Educational Research Association Social Justice in Education Award, the Chapman University Paulo Freire Education Project Social Justice Award, and the National Association for Multicultural Education Exceptional Service Award.

Miguel Zavala, PhD., is associate professor and director of the Urban Learning Program in the Charter College of Education at California State University, Los Angeles. His research interests center on decolonizing and Freirean pedagogies, critical literacies, and their intersection in social movements. His projects include work with and alongside teachers, youth, and parents using ethnic studies and participatory action research, and in seeding critical literacy projects serving immigrant children. His most recent publications include *Rethinking Ethnic Studies* (with C. E. Sleeter, R. T. Cuauhtin, & W. Au), and *Raza Struggle and the Movement for Ethnic Studies: Decolonial Pedagogies, Literacies, and Methodologies,* a historical and ethnographic account of ethnic studies practices. Over the last 2 decades he has been integral to the formation of teacher-led grassroots political education and has nurtured education spaces serving immigrant and Chicanx families in Southern California. Since 2011 he has served on the Board of the California Chapter of the National Association for Multicultural Education (CA-NAME).